Everything has its season, and there is a time for everything under the heaven...

—KOHELET 3:1

JEWISH

RITA MILOS BROWNSTEIN

HOLIDAY

PHOTOGRAPHY BY SHAFFER/SMITH

STYLE

TEXT
DONNA WOLF KOPLOWITZ

FOOD
STACEY STOLMAN WEBB

ILLUSTRATION
SUSAN BLUBAUGH

SIMON & SCHUSTER

Simon & Schuster
Rockefeller Center

1230 Avenue of the Americas
New York, NY 10020

Designed by Rita Milos Brownstein

Manufactured in the United States of America

10 8 6 4 5 7 9

Library of Congress Cataloging-in-Publication Data
Brownstein, Rita Milos, date
Jewish Holiday Style/Rita Milos Brownstein;
photography, Shaffer/Smith; text, Donna Wolf Koplowitz;
food, Stacey Stolman Webb; illustration, Susan Blubaugh.
p. cm.
Includes bibliographical references and index
1. Fasts and feasts—Judaism. 2. Cookery, Jewish. 3. Holiday cookery. 4. Jewish crafts.
I. Koplowitz, Donna Wolf. II. Title.
BM690. B77 1999   99-20723
745.594'1—dc21   CIP

ISBN 0-684-84959-3

THIS BOOK IS DEDICATED TO MY PARENTS

MARGIT AND HOWARD MILOS

WHO SURVIVED THE UNIMAGINABLE:
THE HOLOCAUST

AND IN MEMORY OF THE LOVED ONES
WHO PERISHED:
RACHEL YOSOWITZ
YOSEF YOSOWITZ
HERSHEL YOSOWITZ
LEAH-GITTEL YOSOWITZ

CONTENTS

WHY HOLIDAYS?

The celebration of holidays is such a common practice among humankind that we rarely if ever stop to think, Just what is the purpose of a holiday, anyway? After all, why is the past, which is long gone, a cause for celebration now? ✳ Judaism answers this question by pointing out that the Jewish holidays are not simply marks on the yearly calendar, but a spiral by which we travel to the spiritual coordinates of the holiday time and time again. We are not merely commemorating a historical event and perpetuating our heritage—we are reliving it in our present reality. ✳ What does this really mean? After all, we are not required to go on a group tour to Egypt every Passover to relive the Exodus. However, if we analyze this concept from the perspective of Jewish mysticism/kabbalah, we find that just as every person has a soul, so too does every event. Every event has a special and unique inner spiritual quality and energy. Thus each holiday has something different to offer us. ✳ Passover is well known as the quintessential holiday of freedom and liberation. And what it has to offer us is of immense value: actual assistance in overcoming and effecting redemption from our own personal internal bonds and limitations. For certainly recalling the historical event is both uplifting and inspiring. Although this is true, it is only the starting point. Just as the sun shines more strongly on some days than on others, so does God make the special spiritual quality and energy of each holiday (in this case Passover) shine more strongly in the world during the actual time of the holiday. Thus what we are offered during the days of Passover each year is the opportunity to actually plug into and "download" the energy of this holiday's essence. Every Passover the power of liberation is there to help each one of us attain an ever higher level of our own true personal and spiritual potential as we cross the path of this beam of energy farther up the spiral stairway each year. ✳ The same applies to every Jewish holiday, for each has its own quality and energy waiting for us to access. To do so we need to make our celebration a personal event, hence the importance of customs—personal, familial, and communal. This book serves that purpose by using all the senses to open arenas for the expression of the spirit of the holidays, from the food we eat to the way we beautify the mitzvot (precepts) of each holiday. Above all, this book assists us to bring our own gift of beauty to each of the holidays, as did Miriam and Moses when they led the Jewish people in singing, "This is my God and I will praise him with beauty"(from the Song of the Sea).

Rabbi Shlomo Yaffe
West Hartford, Connecticut

INTRODUCTION

This book is a project of the heart. The concept grew out of my own desire to make the Jewish holidays as beautiful and aesthetically pleasing as possible for my family and friends. ✴ Using my hands to enhance my surroundings has always been my passion. When my husband, Michael, and I began studying Hasidic philosophy, I was surprised and delighted to learn that my whole approach to home style is an example of what is called *hiddur mitzvah*. This is the act of going that extra step to make everything in life as beautiful and as special as possible. ✴ In Judaism, since the spiritual and the physical are intimately connected, each has the power to enhance and infuse vitality into the other, creating a divine partnership. This concept of beauty and spirituality is most attainable during the Jewish holidays. The holiest of times brings out the best in us, compelling us to make our small corner of the world the most special place to be. They envelop our loved ones like a beautiful, rich cloak of happiness, of wonder. ✴ If food is love, then so is a wonderful sukkah and a most perfect golden *etrog*, the most sumptuous of buffets, the brightest and most captivating Chanukah decorations. Love is also a handsome New Year's card that begs to be saved, a set of beeswax menorah candles straight from your kitchen, a clever *shalach manot* food gift for Purim, and a Rosh Hashanah goodie bag to send home with each of your guests. These special touches are perfect examples of *hiddur mitzvot*, those efforts from the heart. ✴ This book, then, is a gift—to my family, to my friends, to you, and to my Creator. It is my humble way of saying thank you for the ability to create joy and beauty and the opportunity to share. ✴ Perhaps the perfect table setting won't change the world, but if this book provides the reader with even a small measure of inspiration to unlock the talent needed to create special holiday beauty throughout the Jewish year, I will be most gratified. Because when the door is unlocked, we are all one step closer to *hiddur mitzvah*— and a life of beauty, both physical and spiritual.

*Pomegranates, the traditional first fruit of the
New Year, are served to remind us to be as abundant
in good deeds as they are in seeds.*

ROSH HASHANAH

THE BLAST OF THE SHOFAR IS THE SIGNAL—the alarm—that the Days of Awe, the ten-day period from Rosh Hashanah to Yom Kippur, has begun. This is a time of serious introspection and soul-searching, because everything done during this time period can affect the outcome of the year to come. It is a time to heal hurts, offer apologies, mend misunderstandings, and right wrongs. It is also a time to increase acts of kindness and charity. If our efforts are undertaken with a sincere heart, then God will look on us favorably and inscribe us in the Book of Life for another year. This process, called *teshuvah*, which means "return," allows us to return to our best true selves and to embark on the New Year with a clean slate. ✴ The Days of Awe begin with Rosh Hashanah, meaning literally the "head of the year," on the first of Tishrei. It is the crown jewel of the Jewish calendar, marking the beginning of the Jewish New Year and the birthday of the world. ✴ Rosh Hashanah is a delicious time of families and friends coming together. Family meals. Crunchy apple slices dipped in honey, as wishes for a sweet New Year. Fat, fragrant round challahs, sometimes studded with sweet raisins, just begging to be pulled apart and passed around. Kosher markets struggle to fill the many orders for fresh briskets of beef, and granddaughters thumb through old recipes for tzimmes, the Ashkenazi sweet potato, prune, and carrot side dish. Pomegranates, the traditional first fruit, are served so that we may do as many good deeds as there are seeds within the fruit. ✴ The Jewish world is bright and joyous; even the fruits and vegetables served are vividly hued—oranges, carrots, the many varieties of apples. Whatever traditions you opt to embrace or decide to create, make sure your Rosh Hashanah is bright, light, and sweet.

NEW YEAR CARDS

This is one of the holidays during which Jewish people send greeting cards to friends and family. Card companies have gotten much more creative in recent years with their Rosh Hashanah cards, selling them singly or by the pack, but why not try your hand at making your family's own? They're much more personal, and recipients will treasure them more, knowing the effort and creativity that went into each card.

New Year's cards may be sent before Rosh Hashanah up until the beginning of Sukkot, so you have a couple of weeks to get them into the mail. Ours are made from both blank cards from the stationery store and colored paper that can be cut to the desired size. Quality art supply stores also sell hand-made papers, some with flower petals or fiber pieces pressed right in. They're a beautiful canvas for handmade cards.

Photographs
(Bottom and opposite page, top left)
Since sending New Year's greetings is a lovely way to stay in touch, you might consider a photo card. Cut a shape in the center of your card with an X-Acto blade for the photo to peek through, as we've shown here. Crop the photo in an interesting way to get close-ups of your subjects—you really don't need to see the furniture in the room or your kids' knees. The honey bottle was borrowed from the children, crowned with an apple hat, then snapped with an ordinary Instamatic camera. The photo was taken to the quick print center, color copied, cut out paper-doll-style, and mounted inside the border between the words of the greeting. Make up your own favorite shot—your children with their arms filled with apples would be charming, taken outdoors on a sunny fall day.

Papier-mâché Apple
(Opposite page, top right)
Just for fun, a tiny papier-mâché apple, available by the dozen in craft and seasonal shops, is tagged with your holiday message, popped into a tiny mailing tube, and sent as an unexpectedly charming Rosh Hashanah greeting.

Writing with Paint Pens
(Opposite page, bottom right)
Gold and silver metallic pens are truly magic. They can transform an ordinary sheet of paper into an elegant, personalized card that's too pretty to throw away. Just draw or write your message across the front in metallic ink—dark papers work well for contrast. Here, we've repeated *L'Shanah Tovah* on one card and drawn a simple autumn leaf pattern on another. For a personal message over your design, write it on contrasting paper and spray-mount or glue-stick into place.

Clip Art
(Above and opposite page, bottom left)
The illustrations in old books and clip art books make wonderful card ideas, and they're easier to reproduce than you think. Just photocopy the illustration to the size you'd like, add type from a personal computer (or hand letter it yourself), and photocopy onto colored paper. If you're not sure how to get it through the copier straight, ask your local print shop to help.

OPEN HOUSE BUFFET

Our Rosh Hashanah open house buffet is short on prep time, long on pleasure. The spirit of the Jewish New Year permeates your home. The talk is relaxed and unhurried. The food is abundant yet simple. And a menu like this allows you to enjoy this special time with the people you love, not careening back and forth from the kitchen to the dining room. Here, we've created ideas for an easily elegant buffet table, headlining food that needn't be eaten at a sit-down meal, foods prepared days ahead, using a vibrant tumble of vegetables from the summer's rich harvest.

We've loaded our table with garden treasures: a heady eggplant dip, a mélange of crudités, and traditional challah-turned-bruschetta. The cognac-laced chopped liver is a dense, surprisingly delicious treat, and tiny apple honey tartlets blend the season's celebrity fruit with the symbolic sweetness of honey. Consider jugs of cold local cider, and keep a crock of long cinnamon sticks nearby.

Some extra perks for you: Except for the tartlets, the foods on our buffet needn't be heated, totally eliminating panic time. This is intentional—Rosh Hashanah services at different synagogues end at different times, which means that your guests don't arrive en masse. Each element of this light luncheon falls into the finger food category—enough to satisfy, never to overfill, since many of your guests will be going on to traditional multicourse family dinners later in the day.

The setting is up to you, but we've chosen earthy autumn colors. As a centerpiece, you might want to use pomegranates—a seasonal "first fruit"—in an attractive glass bowl. These dry beautifully and look great in the house all year long. If your buffet is set up in a room with a fireplace, try this for the mantle—scoop out a large oblong gourd or overgrown zucchini, tuck in some florists' foam, and insert bittersweet.

If you live near a body of fresh running water that contains fish, take a walk after the meal to experience *tashlich*. This is the ceremony of reciting prayers and throwing bread crumbs into the water as a symbolic casting away of our transgressions so we might make a fresh start for the New Year. This ceremony teaches us that, just as a fish's eyes are always open, so is God always watching over us and waiting for us to resolve that we will not repeat our sins. Then, like the water, our sins will also move on. *Tashlich* is a beautiful tradition, and one that children especially love. Adults find something very cleansing about the ceremony, which binds us to nature and reminds us that we are all part of the Creator's world.

M E N U
HERBED CHALLAH BRUSCHETTA
COGNAC CHOPPED LIVER
MEDITERRANEAN EGGPLANT SPREAD
HARVEST TOMATO COMPOTE
ROASTED BEET RELISH
APPLE AND HONEY TARTLETS
NANA'S BASIC MANDEL BREAD
CRUDITÉS WITH DIP

HERBED CHALLAH BRUSCHETTA

SERVES 8–10

1 large challah
1 cup extra-virgin olive oil
2 tablespoons Italian seasoning
2 teaspoons kosher salt
1 teaspoon cracked black pepper

1. Preheat oven to 400°F.
2. Cut challah into ½-inch slices and cut each slice diagonally into 4 pieces.
3. Mix oil, seasoning, salt, and pepper in a small bowl. Place challah on a baking sheet and brush the pieces with the oil mixture. Bake for 5–8 minutes or until golden. Turn pieces over and brush remaining side. Bake for an additional 3–4 minutes or until golden. Remove from oven and cool. Repeat with remaining pieces.

SUGGESTIONS
• Any type of challah will work. We prefer a pullman style because you get even pieces.
• This can be made ahead of time and kept in an airtight container or Ziploc bag.
• Any type of dried seasoning will work, such as sage, thyme, rosemary, or chives.

COGNAC CHOPPED LIVER

MAKES 2 CUPS

1 pound chicken livers
  Kosher salt
3 tablespoons olive oil
¾ cup minced shallots
1 teaspoon minced garlic
¼ cup plus 1 tablespoon cognac
2 hard-boiled eggs
2 tablespoons chopped parsley
2 tablespoons chopped chives
  Salt and pepper to taste

1. Preheat broiler to high.
2. Chicken livers need to be kashered—salt livers on all sides. Place on a broiler pan, on a screen-type rack so that blood can drip off.
3. Broil chicken livers for 4–5 minutes or until blood has exuded. Wash salt away.
4. Heat 2 tablespoons of oil in a large sauté pan. Sauté shallots for 6–8 minutes or until golden. Add garlic and cook for 30 seconds. Add chicken livers and ¼ cup cognac. Let simmer for 12–15 minutes over medium-high heat, until liquid has evaporated and livers are cooked through.
5. Transfer mixture to a food processor fitted with a steel blade. Process liver mixture, eggs, and remaining oil until smooth. Remove mixture to a bowl and fold in parsley and chives. Splash with 1 tablespoon cognac. Season with salt and pepper to taste. Refrigerate for 1 hour.
6. Serve with herbed challah bruschetta.

MEDITERRANEAN EGGPLANT SPREAD

SERVES 6–8

1 large eggplant
4 cloves roasted garlic
1 tablespoon lemon juice
2 tablespoons olive oil
2 tablespoons pitted, chopped Kalamata olives
2 tablespoons chopped sun-dried tomatoes, packed in oil
¼ cup chopped fresh parsley
  Salt and pepper to taste
  Matzo crackers

1. Preheat grill or broiler. Place whole eggplant on grill or under broiler, turning often, until all sides are charred. Cool eggplant, peel skin, and remove pulp.
2. In a food processor fitted with a steel blade, process eggplant, garlic, lemon juice, and olive oil until smooth. Fold in olives, sun-dried tomatoes, and parsley. Season with salt and pepper. Cover and chill for 30 minutes.
3. Serve with matzo crackers.

HARVEST TOMATO COMPOTE

SERVES 8-10

This can be made in advance and frozen. Omit the herbs when cooking and add just before serving.

2 tablespoons olive oil
1½ cups diced red onions
2 cloves garlic, minced
3 pounds ripe tomatoes, peeled, seeded, and diced
⅓ cup shredded basil
⅓ cup chopped parsley
2 tablespoons chopped oregano
2 tablespoons capers
2 tablespoons balsamic vinegar
  Salt and pepper to taste

1. Heat a large sauté pan with oil, add onions, and cook for 2–3 minutes. Add garlic and tomatoes and cook for 15–18 minutes or until most of the liquid has evaporated.
2. Stir in herbs and capers; cook until heated through.
3. Splash with vinegar and season with salt and pepper.

SUGGESTIONS
• Serve with toasted challah.
• Substitute half yellow tomatoes if in season.

ROASTED BEET RELISH

SERVES 8–10

5 large beets (approximately 3 pounds), tops removed and scrubbed
¼ cup vegetable oil
  Salt and pepper to taste
2 large navel oranges
1 teaspoon chopped orange zest
½ cup sliced scallions
1 tablespoon chopped fresh tarragon
2 tablespoons raspberry vinegar
1½ teaspoons Dijon mustard
⅓ cup olive oil
2 tablespoons chopped parsley

1. Preheat oven to 400°F. Line a baking dish with aluminum foil.
2. Toss beets in vegetable oil. Season with salt and pepper and place in baking dish. Roast in preheated oven for 1 hour 15 minutes or until beets are fork tender. Remove and cool.
3. Peel beets and cut into small dice. Place in a large mixing bowl. Remove the skin and membrane of the oranges, cut into sections, and dice. Add oranges, orange zest, scallions, and tarragon to beets. Toss to combine.
4. In a small bowl, whisk together vinegar and mustard. Slowly whisk in olive oil, fold in parsley, and season with salt and pepper. Pour over beet mixture and toss to coat. Cover and chill for 1 hour or overnight if desired.

SUGGESTIONS
• Serve with pita or toasted challah.
• Beet will stain your hands badly, so wear rubber gloves.

APPLE AND HONEY TARTLETS

MAKES 36 TARTLETS

This can be made ahead and frozen.

8 tablespoons margarine
4 Granny Smith apples, peeled, cored, and diced
1 teaspoon ground cinnamon
½ cup honey
½ cup chopped walnuts
¼ cup currants
12 sheets phyllo dough, defrosted

1. Preheat oven to 375°F.
2. Heat a large pan with 2 tablespoons margarine. Sauté apples over medium-high heat for 4–5 minutes or until slightly golden and soft. Add cinnamon and honey and continue cooking for 1–2 minutes. Remove from heat and stir in walnuts and currants. Cool mixture slightly.
3. Melt remaining margarine. On a clean work surface, place down one sheet of phyllo. Brush liberally with margarine and repeat with 3 more sheets, brushing the top sheet. Cut phyllo into 12 even pieces. Place margarine side of each square down in a minimuffin tin.
4. Fill each square with a heaping teaspoon of filling. Gather the sides of the squares in the center (as if you were making a beggar's purse) and push down to seal.

Repeat with remaining phyllo and filling.
5. Bake for 15–18 minutes or until golden. Serve warm.

SUGGESTIONS

• When working with phyllo, keep unused dough well covered so as not to dry out.
• Always defrost phyllo overnight in the refrigerator.
• We usually buy 2 boxes of phyllo when making a recipe because sometimes you get a box where the dough is stuck together.
• If you freeze tartlets, reheat them on a baking sheet in a 400°F oven for 10–12 minutes or until warm.

NANA'S BASIC MANDEL BREAD

MAKES A LOT

Because of the large quantity, this freezes beautifully!

7 large eggs
1⅔ cups sugar
1½ cups vegetable oil
2 tablespoons orange juice
Juice of 1 lemon
8 cups all-purpose flour
2 tablespoons plus 1 teaspoon baking powder
8 ounces chopped walnuts

TOPPING

¼ cup sugar
1 tablespoon ground cinnamon

1. Preheat oven to 350°F.
2. In a large bowl combine eggs, sugar, oil, and juices. In a separate bowl mix together flour, baking powder, and walnuts. Fold dry ingredients into wet and mix until combined.
3. Shape into 5 even logs and place on an ungreased jelly-roll pan. Bake for 35–40 minutes or until golden.
4. In a small bowl mix sugar and cinnamon. Cut logs into ½-inch slices and dip in cinnamon-sugar. Place standing up on a baking sheet and bake for 10–15 minutes. Turn oven off and let stand for a few hours.

Rosh Hashanah treats to end the perfect buffet. Delicate-looking Apple and Honey Tartlets and a basket of Nana's basic mandel bread.

HONEY TASTING

A new twist for Rosh Hashanah: the honey tasting. Set up a separate table at your open house buffet just for honey tasting. We had some fun with the table covering—using a permanent-ink pad from the craft store to rubber stamp plain, inexpensive fabric (unbleached muslin is perfect) with a whimsical bee stamp. Beautiful jars of flavored honeys share the table with honey straws for the children, baskets of challah chunks (plain and raisin), and bowls of apples. Use a variety of apples for color and taste—green Granny Smiths, red Macs, yellow Delicious, blushing Fujis. Remember to keep accompaniments simple and of a fairly neutral flavor—to serve as palate cleansers between one honey and the next. Serve with big mugs of dark-roast coffee.

Above: A sweet reminder of a decidedly different party. Fill clear favor bags with dainty lady apples, honey spoons, a small jar of honey, and perhaps some sesame seed candy. Tie bags with raffia or ribbon and heap into a big basket or pottery bowl by the front door. A wonderful *L'Shanah Tovah.* *Opposite page:* The sweetest party of the New Year, starring a golden rainbow of honeys to taste and compare. Shop your local gourmet store for honey straws for the children, and find as many different honeys as you can for tasting.

The tastes of honey are heady, complex, and varied. Gourmet shops, natural-food stores, and farmer's markets in recent years have begun to offer dozens of honeys that vary in flavor and texture from sunny and light to dark, dense, and rich, some even with hues of red and green. The differences in taste, texture, and color depend on the kind of nectar the bees have been collecting, and there are as many subtle flavors of honey as there are plant nectar sources. (A little nature trivia with which to dazzle your guests: Did you know that a bee must tap the nectar of two million flowers to produce one pound of honey?) Finally, stump your kosher-conversant friends with the fact that honey is the only kosher food that comes from a nonkosher animal. The reason for this? The bee is concentrating flower nectar into honey for the hive—honey is not a product of the bee's body.

Now for the handling of honey. Temperature is very important. The delicate bouquet and fine flavor of honey are vulnerable to heat and improper storage. Excessive heat should be avoided—the damaging effects of heat on honeys can produce an "off" flavor. Store at room temperature out of direct sunlight, or the liquid honey will become granulated. If this happens, simply microwave for two or three minutes, stirring every thirty seconds or so, until the honey is smooth again, good as new.

A BRIEF HONEY PRIMER

Orange Blossom Honey
This honey is found everywhere, with a mild taste and golden color. Many of these honeys come from the nectars of tropical citrus trees, including orange, grapefruit, and tangerine, and most of these honeys are produced in Texas, Florida, and California.

Dandelion Honey
Strong, aromatic, and bright yellow in color, this honey comes from the basic backyard dandelion plant.

Eucalyptus Honey
A strongly flavored, robust honey that comes from the eucalyptus tree, an Australian import. This honey is produced mostly in California and the South.

Clover Honey
This is one of the most commercially popular of all honeys. With a mild taste and a brandy coloring, it comes from the red, white, and sweet yellow clover vetches, or tiny blossoms.

Alfalfa Honey
This comes from Canada and the United States. Mild and light, alfalfa honey is one of the most commonly sold commercial varieties.

Black Locust Honey
Strong, aromatic, and very bright yellow in color, this honey comes from the black locust plant.

Each Yom Kippur, we ask God to grant us another year
of life and good health by sealing our names in
the "book of life" for the coming year.

YOM KIPPUR

THINK OF IT AS A DAY SPA FOR THE SOUL. Immerse yourself in the too rare opportunity to get in touch with the things that really matter: the overhaul of friendships, the love of family, acts of kindness, and the balm of forgiveness. In short, make things right. ✷ Yom Kippur, which falls on the tenth of Tishrei, frees us from all material concerns, and we can concentrate on prayer. Feel the power of millions of Jews the world over, reciting the same prayers, hearing the same melodies. Feel the powerful collective spirit of the millions who went before you on this sacred day throughout the ages. Be a part of the tradition—the spiritual glue that holds Jews together. ✷ Make your meal before the fast a light, pure one, unencumbered by too much salt or heavy spice. Remind your guests that it is said that the mitzvah of eating this meal is as great as the mitzvah of fasting itself. Fresh fruits, light pastas, steamed fishes, and fragrant, just baked challah are appropriate offerings—not too heavy yet satisfying. After the meal, everyone heads to the synagogue for the Kol Nidre service, where it is a tradition to wear white as a symbol of purity, of starting over. ✷ This year, don't think of fasting only as a nuisance or hardship. Instead realize its purpose as a feast for the spirit. Fasting places us in a humble state in which we can more easily identify the areas within us that need improvement. If one performs the ritual fast but fails to gain such insights, the purpose of the day has not been fulfilled. ✷ It is said that God created the world for a purpose, and each one of us has a special role designed to make the world a better place. Think of your role within this plan, and gather strength and light from the Neilah service, the final prayer service of the day. During the entire service, the doors of the Torah Ark are open wide, to signify to us that the gates of heaven are open to all of us at this time. The synagogue is bright and crowded, the gleam of silver Torah adornments and white holiday covering creates an almost heavenly light. The crowd is stirring, waiting for the final blast of the shofar. When it comes, give yourself up to the embraces and greetings of neighboring worshipers and the first sweet taste of honey cake in the synagogue social hall. ✷ Then it's off to officially break the fast.

ACCOMPLISHMENT BOOK

The Book of Life is open during the ten days between Rosh Hashanah and Yom Kippur. During these days, the open book gives us all a chance to make and keep resolutions. It is an ambitious task, but it needn't be daunting. We've created a lovely, personal way to make the message of *teshuvah* and self-realization meaningful to your family and friends.

The Accomplishment Book is a personal collection of tangible promises that everyone writes from the heart. These small, beautiful, blank books, bound with ribbon or raffia and paired with a pen, will be put at each place setting at the meal before the Kol Nidre service, before the fast. You've provided a permanent way for all the guests to record their spiritual wish list—their hopes, dreams, and goals for the coming year and those things that need improvement. It is important to note that these are not mere resolutions—each vow must also contain specifics to make them become reality. For example, if you would like to spend an extra half hour with your children each day, and you feel that story time before lights out is the solution, then list it.

World peace, the dean's list, a healthy family—it all goes into the book. You'll be surprised how special this new tradition becomes. As your guests are about to leave, make sure they take their books with them. During the course of the year, an occasional glance inside will be both a wonderful way to stay inspired and to recall this evening.

The Accomplishment Book is fairly simple to make. Check art supply and stationery stores for interesting papers—heavy stock for front and back covers, lighter weights for the inside pages. Beautiful choices include the marbleized papers with their swirls of beautiful, offbeat pastel tones, and the heavy, handmade papers that have flower petals pressed into the paper composition. The title of the book can be set with a personal computer or hand lettered, if you wish. Calligraphy looks beautiful, but calligraphy felt-tipped pens give you the look without the lessons. For the cutting: Get a print shop to cut your paper, both cover and text weights, to your specifications—they'll usually charge per cut. However, if you have a steady hand, a straight-edge ruler, an X-Acto knife, and a reliable cutting board (we like the self-healing rubber mats), you may do your own cutting. Size is up to you. Five by five inches is fine and is a manageable "favor-size" accessory at a place setting. Six inside pages will probably be enough. In fact, you may want to give everyone a mental nudge by providing page headings—"I wish I hadn't...," "This year, I'd really like to...," and the like. For the binding, punch a few holes and thread with grosgrain ribbons, leather, or

raffia for a more earthy and natural look. Tie on a silky tassel or a few charms from an import store, and either prop against the water goblet or on each person's plate.

A tradition is born. Create Accomplishment Books for your family and friends to fill in during the meal before the fast. Into these books go each guest's spiritual wish list for the year to come.

BREAK THE FAST

This buffet is fun. Everyone is feeling wonderful, and everyone is starved, the perfect combination for a successful meal. At the conclusion of Yom Kippur, the havdalah prayer is recited over a cup of wine, and a festive meal is served.

It is the custom in many Jewish communities to invite friends over for this break-the-fast meal, usually featuring dairy foods and smoked fishes. Bagels are king at this festive gathering, presliced (by you) and heaped high in baskets along the buffet table. Fragrant noodle kugels feature sour cream and applesauce as sidekicks. Fresh fruit platters or salads, smoked-fish plates, and cream cheeses are perfect, prep-free choices. We've added a poached salmon with creamy dill sauce as a nouveau cousin to the traditional smoked sables, lox, and whitefish. Greet your guests as they arrive with the rich scent of just baked coffee cake, hot from the oven, served with creamy cinnamon butter and a pot of steaming coffee.

Although we are celebrating the conclusion of Yom Kippur by breaking the fast, it is a custom for Jews all over the world to begin preparing for the next holiday this same night. Although Sukkot starts five days after Yom Kippur, have your break-fast guests join you in putting at least one piece of the sukkah in place, such as a board or nail, so that they can share with you, in going from mitzvah to mitzvah and strength to strength.

Fasting means more than charity, and the reason is this: The man who fasts does it with his body, the charitable only gives cash.

—TALMUD, SHABBAT

Easy does it. After a day of fasting, it's best to keep your break-the-fast buffet on the light side. Here, we've featured a warm noodle kugel studded with dried cranberries as a surprise instead of the standard raisins, smoked fish platters, a chilled salmon with creamy dill sauce, fresh fruits, and a warm coffee cake fresh from the oven. The coffee cake batter is easy to toss together, baking time is relatively short, and nothing greets your hungry guests like the aroma of freshly baked coffee cake. Another tip: Buy your bagels as fresh as possible, freeze them immediately in plastic bags, and heat them in the oven before your guests arrive. You might consider minibagels instead of the regular size.

Coffee is the drink of choice. And with a houseful of caffeine-deprived guests, we suggest several carafes of different blends. Offer a tea sampler, too, with lots of flavors to choose from. Herbals are popular, and so are the fruit/spice blends. Fresh juices are appropriate, especially after a fast. Float thin lemon and lime slices in pitchers of iced water. When everyone has gathered, offer a toast to your guests with one of the excellent new kosher champagnes that are readily available in larger wineshops. Remember, the icier the better, and less is best.

M E N U

PICKLED HERRING IN
CREAM SAUCE

POACHED SALMON
WITH CUCUMBER
DILL SAUCE

NOODLE KUGEL

SMOKED FISH PLATTER
WITH HORSERADISH
CREAM SAUCE

BASKET OF FRESH ROLLS
AND BAGELS

SOUR CREAM CRUMB
COFFEE CAKE

FRESH FRUIT PLATTER

PICKLED HERRING IN CREAM SAUCE
SERVES 8–10

- 2 16-ounce jars pickled herring fillets in wine sauce
- 2 pints sour cream
- 2 cups thinly sliced red onions
- 2 cups sliced scallions
- Juice and zest of 1 lemon
- ⅓ cup sugar
- Lemon slices for garnish

1. Strain and use only the herring. Run under cold water and pat dry; reserve.
2. In a large bowl combine sour cream, red onions, scallions, lemon juice, zest, and sugar. Mix well. Fold in herring and let marinate overnight.
3. When serving, garnish with lemon slices.

POACHED SALMON WITH CUCUMBER DILL SAUCE
SERVES 8

POACHED SALMON
- 1 side of salmon, skinned (approximately 2–2½ pounds)
- ½ cup chopped shallots
- 2 sprigs fresh dill
- 1 lemon, thinly sliced
- Cracked black pepper
- 1 cup dry vermouth or white wine
- 2 cups vegetable stock or fish stock
- 1 cup water

CUCUMBER DILL SAUCE
- 1 European cucumber, peeled, seeded, diced and drained
- ¼ cup mayonnaise
- ¼ cup sour cream
- ¼ cup chopped fresh dill
- 2 teaspoons lemon juice
- Salt and pepper to taste

1. Cut salmon into 1½-inch strips. In a large sauté pan with deep sides and a tight-fitting cover, sprinkle shallots in pan and top with dill, lemon slices, and cracked pepper. Lay pieces of salmon on top and pour vermouth, stock, and water over salmon.
2. Bring to a boil, reduce to a simmer. Cover and cook for 10–12 minutes or until salmon starts to flake. (Or you can stick in a 350°F oven for 18–20 minutes.)
3. Remove salmon, strain liquid, and cool. Place salmon in a baking dish with reserved liquid. Cover and refrigerate overnight.
4. To prepare cucumber dill sauce: Combine all ingredients in a bowl. Cover and chill overnight.
5. When serving, remove salmon from liquid. Place on platter and garnish with fresh dill and lemon. Serve with cucumber dill sauce.

NOODLE KUGEL
MAKES ONE 9 × 13-INCH PAN
This is a traditional sweet kugel with dried cranberries taking the place of raisins.

- 4 ounces whipped cream cheese
- 1 pound cottage cheese
- 1 pint sour cream
- 5 large eggs
- ½ cup granulated sugar, divided
- ½ pound unsalted butter, melted and divided into two equal parts
- ½ teaspoon nutmeg
- 1 pound wide egg noodles, cooked
- 1 cup dried cranberries
- 2 cups cornflake crumbs

1. Preheat oven to 350°F. Grease a 9 × 13-inch glass baking dish.
2. In the bowl of an electric mixer, beat together cream cheese, cottage cheese, and sour cream. Mix until well incorporated. Add eggs one at a time until thoroughly mixed. Add ¼ cup sugar, ¼ pound melted butter, and nutmeg. Gently fold in cooked noodles and cranberries. Pour mixture into prepared pan, reserve.
3. In a small bowl, combine cornflake crumbs, remaining melted butter, and remaining sugar. Mix until coated. Cover noodle mixture with topping and bake for 1 hour or until topping is golden brown and filling begins to bubble. Cool before serving.

HORSERADISH CREAM SAUCE
MAKES 2 CUPS

- 1 cup sour cream
- ¾ cup mayonnaise
- ½ cup prepared horseradish (use white horseradish, not red)
- ⅓ cup chopped parsley
- 1 teaspoon Worcestershire sauce
- Salt and pepper to taste

1. In a medium bowl, combine all ingredients; season with salt and pepper.
2. Refrigerate for at least 1 hour or overnight.

SOUR CREAM CRUMB COFFEE CAKE

MAKES ONE 9-INCH CAKE

CRUMB TOPPING

- ¼ cup all-purpose flour
- ⅓ cup brown sugar
- ⅓ cup chopped pecans
- ½ teaspoon ground cinnamon
- 6 tablespoons butter, cut into chunks

BATTER

- 2 cups all-purpose flour
- 1 teaspoon baking powder
- ¼ teaspoon baking soda
- ½ teaspoon salt
- 1 stick unsalted butter
- ¾ cup granulated sugar
- 1 teaspoon pure vanilla extract
- 2 eggs
- 1 cup sour cream

Confectioners' sugar for dusting (optional)

1. Preheat oven to 350°F. Grease and flour a 9-inch cake pan.

2. To prepare crumb topping: In a medium bowl, combine flour, brown sugar, pecans, and cinnamon; mix well. With fingertips, work in butter until evenly distributed; refrigerate.

3. To prepare batter: In a medium bowl, sift together flour, baking powder, baking soda, and salt; set aside.

4. In a large bowl, using an electric mixer, beat together butter, sugar, and vanilla until light and fluffy. Add eggs one at a time until well incorporated. Add flour mixture and sour cream until well incorporated.

5. Spoon mixture into prepared pan and smooth top. Cover with the prepared crumb mixture. Bake for 40–45 minutes or until an inserted toothpick comes out clean. Cool cake on wire rack for 15 minutes, unmold, and cool completely. Dust with confectioners' sugar just before serving, if desired.

Our sour cream crumb coffee cake. Butter, spices, pecans, and sour cream make a classic slice of paradise.

After leaving Egypt, the Jewish people dwelt in the desert and were protected from the harsh elements by the miraculous clouds sent by God. These clouds were the original sukkah.

SUKKOT

OUTDOOR PLEASURES. For those of you who need an occasional reminder to pause and reconnect with the beauty of nature, Sukkot is your holiday. Leaving the confines of our homes to sit in this fragile shelter, with starlight peeking through the porous roof by night and sunlight streaming in by day, we can again feel the wonder of nature. ✳ The clean scent of pine branches overhead, combined with good food, special company, and the almost weddinglike high spirits of this holiday, make Sukkot a thumbs-up favorite on the Jewish calendar. It is an enchanting time for children as they crowd with enthusiasm around the beautifully decorated outdoor "house" crafted of nature's treasures, complete with tables and chairs, special decorations, twinkling night-lights, and good things to eat. Indeed, the mitzvah of eating in the sukkah can be such a captivating experience that even after the meal is over both adults and children alike tend to linger, as if trying to soak up as much of the good feeling as possible. ✳ "The Holiday of Booths": Sukkot is a seven-day festival beginning on the fifteenth of Tishrei, recalling the miraculous way the Jewish people survived for forty years in the harsh Sinai desert after the Exodus from Egypt. It celebrates the gift of the "miraculous clouds of glory" that were always present to shield the several million men, women, and children from the desert sun and sudden sandstorms. And it is a reminder to us that even when not obvious, all forms of sustenance and shelter are ultimately provided by the Creator. ✳ Sukkot falls during the time of the harvest so that its rich bounty can be used to add joy to the holiday, but the real excitement centers around the sukkah—the building, decorating, and week of joyous celebrating within its temporary walls. In some urban areas several neighbors may share a sukkah. In Israeli cities there are rows and rows of sukkot on high-rise apartment house balconies. In New York there are special sukkot on Wall Street and other locations so that Jews who work in Manhattan can fulfill the mitzvah of eating in the sukkah even at lunchtime. ✳ The sukkah hop is a popular tradition among friends and neighbors in many communities. It's great fun—plan your route and make it a progressive dinner. Visit and admire each sukkah as each host serves a course from appetizers to dessert and coffee; you will find it both a physical and spiritual joy.

LULAV AND ETROG

Many stories have been attached to the *lulav* and *etrog*. But first, an explanation. Palm fronds are made into a natural woven holder that contains three of the four required species for the celebration of Sukkot: palm (*lulav*), myrtle, and willow branches. Since the *lulav* is the largest, the unit of three is simply referred to as the *lulav*. The fourth, the *etrog*, is a fragrant citrus fruit grown in Israel that resembles an outsize lemon or lime. Blessings are said while shaking the *lulav* and *etrog* on each day of Sukkot except Shabbat, preferably in the morning. The four species represent different parts of the human body: the *etrog* is the heart; the straight palm is the sturdy spine of the Jewish people; the rounded myrtle leaf is the eye; and the willow leaf is the mouth. This symbolism reminds us to serve God with every part of our being.

The four species are also used to describe different kinds of Jews. The *etrog,* possessing both taste and fragrance, is compared to the person who studies Torah and performs good deeds. The palm has a pleasant taste but no fragrance, and represents one who studies Torah but does not do good deeds. The myrtle has no taste but a pleasant fragrance, resembling one who does not study Torah but does good deeds. And the willow, which has neither taste nor fragrance, is like one who does not study Torah or perform good deeds. When all four species are together, Jews can become united and compensate for shortcomings in others.

On the first day, you shall take the fruit of a beautiful tree, palm branches, myrtle boughs, and willows and rejoice before the Lord.

—VAYIKRA 23:40

Your local Judaica store or synagogue will order *lulav* and an *etrog* for you. If you live near a city with a large Jewish population, you may want to visit an "*etrog* warehouse" to select your own. Everyone tries to buy the most perfect *etrog* for their holiday, to enhance their mitzvah. When the prayer is recited, the *lulav* and *etrog* are shaken in all four directions and up and down, to signify that God is everywhere.

Storing your *lulav* and *etrog* is fairly simple. Most Judaica stores sell a *lulav* case, which is a long plastic tube. This prevents the *lulav* from breaking. Because the willow and myrtle tend to become brown at the tips before the week is over, you might consider buying extras of these. Wrap them in a damp towel, store in the refrigerator, and replace as needed. The *etrog* comes in a cardboard box wrapped in unprocessed wool; keep it here when not in use.

Above: Don't toss your beautiful *etrog* after Sukkot. Rather, try our pomander balls, studded with star anise or cloves, then wrapped in delicate lace or net and tied with gossamer ribbonings. Scent your table linens for an entire sweet year. *Opposite page:* One who fulfills the mitzvah of the *lulav* and *etrog* brings peace and harmony among all the Jewish people.

THE GARDEN SUKKAH

Celebrate the dazzle of the changing seasons. Use your backyard as a vibrant, jewel-toned canvas for your garden sukkah. Harvest long-lasting mums, marigolds, and asters in all their eye-popping splendor, and use these cold-loving beauties lavishly. Flowers in burgundies, golds, bronzes, and yellows mix with the mellow autumn sun, to sift through the wooden lattice arches of your garden sukkah. Coax some ornamental cabbage into big terra-cotta pots. Thread hydrangeas among the cut pine branches that form the sukkah roof for a lush forest feeling. Hook a candelabra from the roof, centered, or scatter tiny tea lights in glass cups all around the interior. They're both magical looks for nighttimes.

On the strictly practical side, since the temperatures can plunge during a fickle fall cold snap, we suggest using a staple gun to attach clear plastic sheeting to the outside of your sukkah. It will keep you quite comfortable and gives the illusion of a greenhouse.

Since dwelling in this temporary shelter as often as possible adds to the mitzvah of observing Sukkot, you may find yourself using your sukkah not just as a dining room, but as a place to sit and read the newspaper with a cup of coffee or tea.

Woven lattice always brings a beautiful garden to mind—of wild roses in a country setting, a tumble of morning glories surging skyward on a neat trellis, as a stately accent along a dignified hedge. Lattice works just as well in your own backyard—it's readily available, inexpensive, and easy to work with. For beauty and durability, stain your lattice walls with a solid-toned oil-based stain. We used a sage green, but white is a classic choice for a pristine look. According to Jewish law, if the wind can blow out a candle in your sukkah, the walls need to be more solid. Try stapling plastic sheets to

The clear autumn sun streams through the wooden lattice-work of the garden sukkah, casting patterns on the patio.

the outside of the walls. If you don't have the time or know-how to cut the gentle, arched entryway, your local handyman can do it quickly for you. If you have a large open deck off the kitchen or family room, the lattice-walled sukkah works well, too, creating a wonderful outdoorsy room that gives you easy access to the kitchen.

Give your interior a luxuriant roof of young pines or branches. We found ours on a walk in the woods after a storm. If you're not near a wild, wooded area, look up a tree farm that specializes in raising evergreens. Fill up your trunk and you'll have enough for a thick, fragrant roof. Hang bunches of dried flowers upside-down from your roof to carry the garden theme, along with a few

bunches of drying herbs for a spicy aroma. Haul over some of your favorite garden statuary and place near the entrance of your sukkah as a welcoming touch.

Dig your own mums from a flower farm, potting them up for accents in and around your sukkah. After the holiday, use them as autumn decorations, flanking your front door. Before the ground freezes, plant them in your perennial beds for fall color, year after year. We choose different colors every year and plant them in one of our raised beds set aside for cutting flowers. Many of our mums were gifts from guests we've invited for Sukkot meals, and they enjoy seeing "their" flowers year after year.

You can create a garden party glow with special light-

ing that won't take up precious table space. Hang your candelabra carefully from a roof pole, taking care to use short votives that won't place the flames too near the greenery. Wall sconces are a bright lighting idea, too, screwed securely into the sukkah wall.

As for the meals you serve in your sukkah, keep things simple so that you can enjoy your guests. Avoid multicourse meals that keep you running back and forth. Rather, use salads and finger foods to serve before a warm, satisfying one-pot cassoulet or a perfect platter of chicken, roasted vegetables, and potatoes, served with red cabbage and an updated Israeli salad with a rainbow of five or six types of beans tossed with balsamic vinegar and olive oil.

SUKKAH BY THE SEA

All right. Maybe you don't have a seashore house with a private beach. But even if you live among the cornfields of Kansas, you can still create a sukkah with a seaside feeling. Use crisp canvas of billowy nylon for the sides, cool blues and greens against white for nautical contrast. Add the sway of dreamy Chinese lanterns and beachcomber shells in your accessories, and you'll practically smell the salt air—wherever you happen to be.

Pot up some pampas or other ornamental grasses for the outside of your sukkah, rather than flowers, to create a beachy mood. Use tiki torches outside—a dramatic way to welcome your guests at night. If you use white nylon sides, tie back your entrance flap for a look of casual elegance. Use hurricane globes to protect your candles from the wind— an inch or two of sand or seashells around the candles look great. Try hot gluing beautiful shells, whimsical sailboat buttons, or ceramic starfish to plain napkin rings. For a finishing touch, scatter extra shells around your table.

Keep it casual—let the blue and white touches say it all.

Again, keep your meals easy: a hearty, creamy fish chowder with crusty bread and a salad for luncheons and your special one-dish casseroles for suppers. Bowls of fresh fruit look lovely and serve as snacks and desserts as well.

A note about using canvas or ripstop nylon for your sukkah walls: Purchase a grommet kit from your local hardware store. Grommets are professional looking, make attaching your walls a snap, and are surprisingly easy to create with just the kit and a hammer.

As refreshing as lunch in a cabana by the sea, no matter where you live, our beach lovers' sukkah features crisp table looks in whites and blues, accented with natural treasures from the deep.

In sukkot [booths] shall you dwell, seven days.—VAYIKRA 23:42

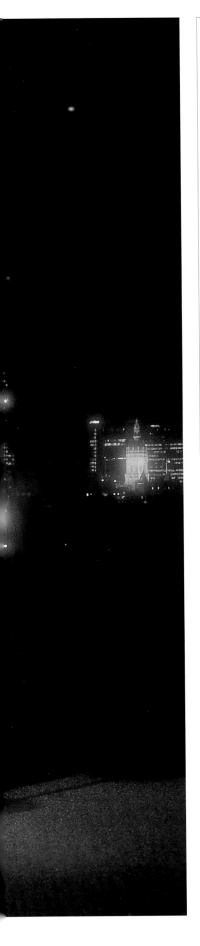

THE PENTHOUSE SUKKAH

A salon in the stars. Surely our rooftop sukkah, surrounded by night sky and city lights, creates a special mood for a unique holiday. High-tech and sleek, with walls created of corrugated fiberglass, our fantasy sukkah is strung simply with silvery beads and accented with tiny white tree lights.

Of course, you don't have to live in a high rise to create the understated elegance of this sukkah style—you can do it just as easily in the suburbs. The walls and roof are easy to store, the furniture is practically weatherproof, and the materials will last for years and years. We see only one problem: The glamour of this ethereal outside dining and reception room will make you wish the holiday of Sukkot lasted lots longer than seven days.

If you live in a high-rise building and have temporary access to the rooftop, the stage is set for your sukkah on top of your world. We used metal walls here for photographic purposes, but metal should not be used, as it could be a lightning hazard. Corregated fiberglass gives a similar appearance and it is recommended. Please make sure all materials used are safe and do not pose a fire hazard from the lighting system. Check with all appropriate authorities such as a fire marshal, town building inspector, etc., to make sure that what you plan to do will be safe. Just remember that all "solid" walls need extra wind support, so consider extra corner brace supports. If you have power for lighting, great. If not, our silvery paint-can lanterns are easy to make and provide ample candle wattage.

Our penthouse sukkah just proves that you can be a city dweller and still fulfill the mitzvah of Sukkot, the "Holiday of Booths," with a unique and definitely different sukkah. Perfect also for the apartment with a small balcony, usually off the living room. The opaque walls give you the luxury of a completely private extra room for meals, guests, conversation, and study. The spare, high-tech look is fine-tuned with simple chairs that don't mind the rain. A pair of topiary trees at the entrance give this sukkah a "can't fail" touch of uptown ambience.

Night-lights. Make these paint-can lanterns to hang in your sukkah. First, ask your paint store to save or sell you some empty paint cans. Fill your cans with water and freeze them overnight. With large nails, hammer holes in the cans, either at random or in a pattern. After melting the ice and draining the water, insert a candle, add three chains and suspend from the roof of your sukkah. A note of caution: Always place candles in glass cups before placing in lanterns so that hot wax can't spill out the holes.

ROOFS

It's almost finished. The roof is the crowning touch to your sukkah and the most important. Whatever you choose to use, remember a few things. The roof covering, or *schach*, is to be temporary, to remind us of the Jews' hasty exit from Egypt. The sukkah is a re-creation of the temporary shelters of our patriarchs; therefore, use no nails, staples, or other nonorganic materials. And while the roof covering must have more shade than light, it should also have enough openings so that the evening stars may be seen.

Roofs can be cut from the ground, or the bamboo mats and poles can be ordered from specialty sukkah outlets either through a synagogue, a Judaica shop, or many of the sources in large metropolitan areas with sizable Jewish populations.

The most traditional coverings are bamboo poles or roll-up mats. The bamboo is handsome and comes in lengths of up to twelve feet. It gives your sukkah a rustic, island look. If you have a garage, the long bamboo poles can be stored easily along a wall with simple bicycle brackets. They also do double duty in the summer garden for pole bean tepees. If you live in a condo or apartment with limited storage, we suggest the woven mats. They can be rolled up and stored easily and neatly. The mats also have a clean, uncluttered, almost Japanese-screen flavor. New York City has many seasonal sukkah outlets, and the suppliers we've used in our resource guide will be happy to ship just about anywhere.

As an alternative, try heaping pine boughs randomly over your roof. The sharp, spicy scent of pine is as lovely as the languid, long armloads of greenery hanging over the sides of your sukkah. If you live in a warmer climate, palm fronds are a cool, striking way

to cover your roof without blocking the stars.

Now for the decorations, a project for everyone in the family. Classic hanging adornments include pretend fruits and tiny colored or white electric lights, but the sky's the limit as far as ideas go. Just make certain that objects attached to your roof hang at least eleven inches down, for according to Jewish law anything higher is considered part of the roof, which must be totally organic.

Save your New Year's cards from friends—cover with clear contact paper to protect them from the rain and hang with yarn. Create fruit and

spice ropes intertwined with small terra-cotta flowerpots for a French country cottage look. Weave fresh flowers into your roof, if you still have them in bloom. If not, hang bunches of dried flowers and herbs upside-down from the roof—elegant, updated naturals to fix a lasting impression. Snip tin stars, suns, and moons, decorated with punchwork, for a celestial theme.

Most important, share the fun and creativity with the ones you cherish. These are the rituals that create the memories, passed through the generations like treasured heirlooms.

Natural harvest: Try a lavish display of dried orange-slice garlands to decorate your sukkah roof. Slice a dozen oranges thinly and bake in a 250°F. oven on the center rack for 2 hours or until dry. Spray with a clear varnish, and string with a thread and needle, alternating with wooden beads in colors or natural wood tones. Apples or lemons work beautifully, too.

Opposite page, clockwise from top left: Bamboo mats make easy-to-store, lightweight roofs with a clean, exotic look. Palm branches, cool and green, provide excellent shade without blocking the evening stars. Bamboo poles are neat, easy to store, and give a streamline look to your roof. Pine branches are rustic, natural, and provide a delicious, spicy smell that invites guests to linger in your seven-day outdoor room.

BUILDING A SUKKAH

B e brave. Your first sukkah will be the most daunting, but follow our guidelines and you'll be the creator of a sukkah to serve your needs. Next year you may find that you'd like to expand or relocate your sukkah—it's fairly easy to adapt these plans. You can, of course, order a prefab canvas or nylon sukkah from a company specializing in easy-up sukkahs, but building your own is much more satisfying than using someone else's ideas. Don't be shy. Get a neighbor or a friend to help; if you have the design and they have the know-how, it's a creative combination. You can even hire a handyman to help out.

Remember some basic do's and don'ts, in keeping with Jewish law. Don't build your sukkah under a tree. You must be able to see the stars through the roof of your sukkah at night, and it's pretty impossible to see under a canopy of leaves as well as your roof. Don't use nails or staples on your roof—organic materials only. Don't turn over the building project to someone else entirely—the rule is that it must be at least partially erected by you.

Now, about the sukkahs we've shown on the previous pages. Believe it or not, they were all made using the same wooden frame. Three totally different looks, one frame. Simply by changing the materials, you can change the walls—all you need is the frame. If you have a wonderful idea for a spatter-painted, Jasper Johns–type canvas sukkah, then simply replace the kit's walls with your own. The possibilities for walls are endless. If you're a fan of Japanese decor, the look of shoji screens can be cleverly copied with opaque fiberglass walls. This means that the look is rice paper, yet the sukkah is waterproof. Clear plastic sheeting is inexpensive and gives your sukkah a greenhouse look. A bonus: You get a view of the outside of your sukkah. If you have access to woods and field with lots of twigs and limbs, you can create a wonderful Adirondack twig-style sukkah. Maybe a local craftsman can help. For a comprehensive listing of companies that sell prefab kits and supplies, see page 138.

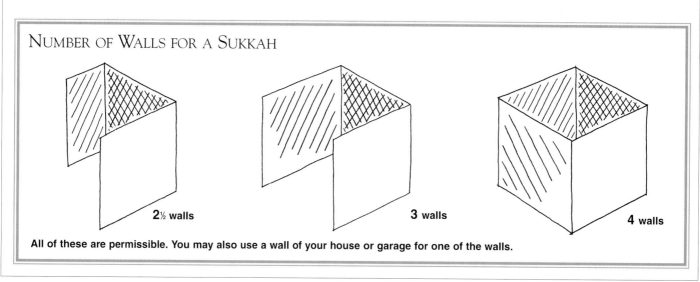

NUMBER OF WALLS FOR A SUKKAH

2½ walls

3 walls

4 walls

All of these are permissible. You may also use a wall of your house or garage for one of the walls.

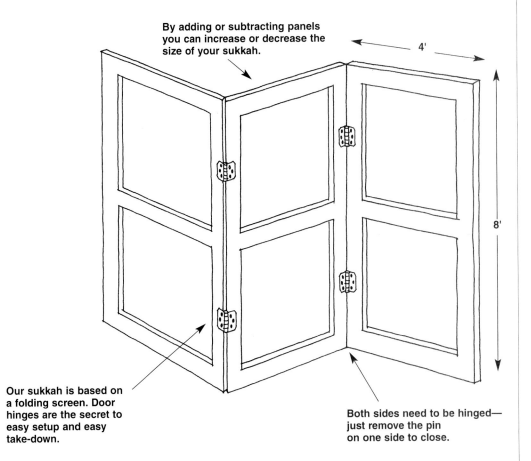

By adding or subtracting panels you can increase or decrease the size of your sukkah.

4'

8'

Our sukkah is based on a folding screen. Door hinges are the secret to easy setup and easy take-down.

Both sides need to be hinged—just remove the pin on one side to close.

LIST OF MATERIALS

2" × 3" × 8' BUILDING STUDS

3" LOOSE-PIN DOOR HINGES

LATTICE

WHITE NYLON OR CANVAS

1" SELF-DRILLING SCREWS

3' × 8' SHEETS CORRUGATED FIBERGLASS

ELECTRIC DRILL WITH SCREWDRIVER TIP

BOLTS AND SCREWS FOR CORNERS

Our eight-by-twelve-foot sukkah seats between ten and twelve people. You may follow the same basic concept by adding or subtracting panels to make it the perfect size for your needs.

The simple secret to easy setup and take-down is hinges. Regular loose-pin door hinges hold each panel together, and when Sukkot is over they simply fold up like a screen and tuck away for easy storage. The panels are simply put together like a frame.

Don't use pressure-treated lumber. It warps very easily and shouldn't be stored inside the house because of the chemicals used to treat it. Also, because of the moisture in pressure-treated lumber, it is harder to work with.

We used one-inch self-drilling screws. You'll save a lot of time, because these go right into the wood without having to start a hole with another tool first. A power drill with a screw tip or an electric screwdriver is a must-have.

Corners may be done in several ways. You could overlap the sides and top by cutting halfway through each one, then overlapping and

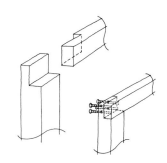

screwing them together.

Another way is to use the "captured" nut-and-bolt method. This is easier than the overlap method but requires more drilling. It also makes a strong corner.

Visit your hardware store for lots of ways to join your corners together, but remem-

½" deep × 1¼" hole to recess head of bolt. Then ⅜" hole × 5½" deep.

1¼" hole to allow placement of nut

5" to center

ber a couple of things. First, the cost of a nut and bolt is about sixty-five cents, while a single bracket may cost several dollars. Second, the mitzvah is to have as many guests and as many meals in the sukkah as possible. And, weather permitting, some people even sleep in it!

*Like water coming down drop by drop and becoming a
great river, so is the Torah.*
—SONG OF SONGS

SIMCHAT TORAH

THE SEASON OF OUR REJOICING. Sukkot is followed immediately by Shmini Atzeret and Simchat Torah, on the twenty-second and twenty-third days of Tishrei. These days are marked with jubilant celebrations as the final portions of the five books of the Torah are completed and the yearly cycle begins all over again. ✳ On Shmini Atzeret we also take leave of the sukkah. Many have the custom of eating a light snack in the afternoon to fulfill the mitzvah of dwelling in the sukkah one last time. Any wistful longing is quickly dispelled with the arrival of Simchat Torah at sunset that very same day. ✳ If ever there was a time of joy and celebration in the synagogue, this is it. All the Torah scrolls are removed from the Ark in their beautiful coverings and marched around the interior of the synagogue in a happy parade complete with clapping, singing, dancing, babies high on fathers' shoulders, and young children waving their parade flags. Ritual and solemn behavior are completely forgotten on this special occasion, as noise and partylike celebration rule. Friends talk and laugh easily and informally, sitting or standing in groups. Everyone kisses the Torahs as they are paraded by, and it is especially fortuitous to kiss as many as possible on as many of the seven rotations as possible. If your synagogue has many Torahs, that can lead to quite a lot of kissing. Tables are usually set up with candy, pastries, and other treats to fuel the marchers. Grown-ups can find extra energy, thanks to a strategically placed "schnapps" table, stocked with spirits and cordials. ✳ The joy of Simchat Torah is considered greater than that of any other holiday, because it celebrates the relationship of the Jewish people to the Torah. Even after the Romans conquered Jerusalem and destroyed the Holy Temple, the Jews took the Torah with them wherever they went in the two thousand years of exile that followed. And the Torah has been so revered that no two Torah scrolls have ever been found to differ in as much as even one letter. While the Jews have kept the Torah in even the most hostile of conditions, perhaps it is more correct to say that it is the Torah, with its infinite wisdom and goodness, that has kept the Jews.

FLAGS

Flag waving may be as American as apple pie, but it's as Jewish as Simchat Torah, too. Children are a special part of this holiday, since the Torah procession originated in the sixteenth century as a way to enable children to feel closer to the Torah. Arm your favorite little ones with our kid-pleasing flags that carry a cache of colorful candies at the top instead of the traditional apple. This ties in with the old tradition of giving sweets after a Talmud lesson so children will always associate sweetness with Torah learning.

Our colorful felt flags are easy to make and much more attractive than the paper flags usually handed out in synagogue for children. These require no sewing, and the children can design and construct the flags easily. The few materials needed can be found at your local craft and hardware stores, and the entire project can be done in an afternoon. Just make sure to tell your children to eat the candy *after* they've marched around with the Torah seven times, and get the toothbrushes lined up afterward!

These no-sew flags are easy to create and great fun to decorate. When choosing your wooden dowels at the lumberyard, hardware outlet, or craft store, buy them a little thicker than you think you need. The filled candy balls might be too heavy for a very slender dowel. Two and a half feet should be plenty of length for each flag, and the dowels are very inexpensive (if you don't save your flags, you can always use the dowels to stake up your tomato plants!).

Cut your flags in rectangles, as shown here, or in pennant-type shapes. Felt is very easy

Fabulous flags lead the Simchat Torah processional with bright colors, terrific trims, and a topping of assorted candy treats.

to cut and never needs hemming. Use pinking shears for a fun look, if you wish. Attach the fabric to the dowels with crafter's glue or Therm O Web's Peel N Stick, which comes in large sheets that attaches to the back of the felt. When you have the correct length, just give it a cut with your scissors. Cut letters out of felt or use puffy paint for your message, usually "Rejoice with the Torah."

Add rickrack, buttons, appliqués, or other treasures from the notions department of your local craft or sewing store. Children can glue their class picture on their flags, too, and "frame" with puffy paint. After Simchat Torah, the flag makes a wonderful wall decoration for a child's room.

Use the lacing stitch with

yarn or embroidery thread to bind the edges of the flags for a decorative look that even children can manage. It's the same concept as the leather key case craft kits and looks extra colorful with a contrasting color.

Now for the candy balls. The two-part clear plastic balls have a tab and hole at the top. Snap off the tab carefully with pliers, and if you have a Dremel tool, use the drill attachment to gently drill holes on the top and bottom pieces of the ball. These holes should be the same size as the dowel for a snug fit. Mount the balls on the dowels (after the flags have been glued on), fill with candies, snap the two pieces together, glue a candy on top for a finished look, and let the parade begin—in style.

LIST OF MATERIALS

FELT, IN SEVERAL BRIGHT COLORS

2½" WOODEN DOWELS

PEEL N STICK GLUE STRIPS OR CRAFTER'S TACKY GLUE

CLEAR PLASTIC ORNAMENT BALLS (AT CRAFT STORES)

NOTIONS:
FANCY TRIM
BUTTONS
YARNS
RICKRACK
PUFFY FABRIC PAINT

FESTIVE MEAL

Stuffed cabbage—the ultimate Jewish comfort food. These plump rolls of meat and rice wrapped in cabbage leaves and simmered in delectable sauces say it all. They evoke memories of warm kitchens with bubbling pots on the stove. Of favorite *bubbies*. A special flowered plate with a chip on the edge, and of secret recipes handed down through the generations. They're a tradition on Simchat Torah because their shape resembles that of a Torah scroll. In that spirit, then, we're headlining this soul-satisfying entrée for our festive meal, the first meal eaten inside after Sukkot.

This is a time for celebration, pure and simple. The table is bright with flags and color. The meal is served in the evening, before going to synagogue for the festivities. This meal is so laced with tradition that it sets the mood for the ages-old traditional festivities to come in the synagogue. Serve it up with high spirits.

Here are two bright variations on the usual stuffed cabbage—a lower-fat version made with ground turkey and a dairy version. The photograph on the opposite page features a classic with a new twist—red cabbage rolls filled with ground turkey and wild rice, flavored with a sweet-and-sour cranberry sauce. To accompany this tangy version, serve egg noodles tossed gently with poppy seeds, lemon zest, and a bit of margarine. A fragrant pear and raspberry cobbler harmonizes the meal.

For vegetarians, we present a delicious marriage of Napa cabbage leaves stuffed with orzo, zucchini, eggplant, pesto, and Parmesan cheese, simmered in a hearty tomato sauce. Cabbage freezes very nicely, so you can make up big batches weeks ahead and heat them up as you need them.

Some cabbage know-how: Savoy cabbage is available everywhere, and the crinkly leaves are very easy to separate for rolling. If you prefer the regular green cabbage, try popping the whole cabbage into the freezer overnight and let it thaw in the morning. You'll find that the limp leaves are very easy to separate, and the taste is not affected at all. Another trick to aid rolling is to place the separated leaves in the microwave for a minute or two on a paper towel with a sprinkling of water. This will make the leaves quite manageable and soften the spines for rolling.

Make some "mini" Simchat Torah flags out of colored index cards and wood skewers. Spike them into Styrofoam in tiny clay pots that you've decorated with paint pens. Or let the children create "flag" place cards for your guests with bright craft foam sheets and craft sticks. Keep the festive spirit with bright colors and contrasting table linens.

Time your meal so that everyone gets off to synagogue in time to see the Torah scrolls being removed from the Ark for their march around the synagogue seven times. Most synagogues will serve *pareve* (nondairy) desserts so that everyone can indulge on this special evening.

Try red cabbage instead of the usual green; turkey and wild rice in place of the traditional ground beef and rice filling; and simmer it in a sweet-and-sour cranberry sauce.

RED CABBAGE ROLLS WITH TURKEY AND DRIED CRANBERRIES

MAKES 10 ROLLS

Use a mixture of white- and dark-meat ground turkey to keep rolls from becoming too dry.

1 red cabbage, approximately 3 pounds
1½ pounds ground turkey
2 cups cooked long grain and wild rice
1 medium onion, chopped
2 cloves garlic, chopped
1⅓ cups dried cranberries
½ teaspoon dried thyme
½ teaspoon salt
½ teaspoon cracked black pepper
1 cup cranberry sauce
1 cup apple juice
½ cup chicken stock
¼ cup brown sugar
2 tablespoons lemon juice

1. Preheat oven to 375°F.
2. Place cabbage in a large pot of boiling water. Gently remove leaves as they become tender, making sure that there are ten good-size leaves. Cook remaining cabbage until tender, drain, chop, and reserve.
3. In a large bowl, combine turkey, rice, onion, garlic, cranberries, thyme, salt, and pepper.
4. In a medium pot, combine cranberry sauce, apple juice, chicken stock, brown sugar, and lemon juice. Bring to a boil, reduce to a simmer, and whisk until smooth; reserve.
5. On a clean work surface, place cabbage leaf down. Trim the core. Place ½ cup mixture on top of each leaf. Fold sides in toward center and roll tightly. Repeat with remaining cabbage leaves and filling. Place rolls in a large oven-safe heavy casserole or sauté pan.

Top with reserved chopped cabbage and sauce. Bring to a boil on top of the stove, cover, and place in preheated oven for 1½ hours. Uncover and cook for 30 minutes or until tender.

A VARIATION ON BOILING THE CABBAGE IN STEP TWO:

• Freeze the cabbage overnight or up to two days. Let thaw overnight. The next day the cabbage will be very limp and easy to work with. This works best for a regular green cabbage or a red cabbage. It is not recommended for Savoy cabbage because the leaves are thin and too delicate for freezing.

LEMON POPPY EGG NOODLES

SERVES 6

1 12-ounce package wide egg noodles
2 tablespoons olive oil
Zest of 1 lemon
2 tablespoons chopped parsley
1 tablespoon poppy seeds
Salt and pepper to taste

1. Prepare egg noodles according to package directions. Drain and reserve.
2. Heat oil in a large sauté pan; add noodles, lemon zest, parsley, and poppy seeds. Toss and cook until heated through. Season with salt and pepper to taste.

VEGETARIAN STUFFED CABBAGE

MAKES 10 ROLLS

1 large head Savoy cabbage
3 tablespoons olive oil, divided
2 cups diced onion, divided
4 cups diced eggplant
1 cup diced yellow squash
1 cup diced zucchini
1 cup diced red pepper
1 cup diced mushrooms
1 cup cooked orzo
6 tablespoons prepared pesto
2 large eggs, beaten
1 teaspoon salt
½ teaspoon black pepper
1 tablespoon chopped garlic
1 35-ounce can whole peeled tomatoes
½ cup dry red wine
1 tablespoon sugar
Salt and pepper to taste

1. Preheat oven to 375°F.
2. Place cabbage in a large pot of boiling water. Gently remove the leaves as they become tender, making sure that there are ten good-size leaves. Cook remaining cabbage until tender, drain, chop, and reserve. This should amount to 1½ cups.
3. Heat 2 tablespoons oil in a large sauté pan. Add 1 cup of onions and cook for 2–3 minutes or until translu-cent. Add eggplant and cook for 3–4 minutes or until soft and golden. Add squash, zucchini, peppers, mushrooms, and reserved chopped cabbage, and continue cooking for 6–8 minutes or until golden and dry. Transfer to a large bowl. Toss with orzo, 5 tablespoons pesto, eggs, salt, and pepper.
4. Heat remaining oil in a medium saucepan. Add remaining 1 cup onions and cook for 1–2 minutes. Add garlic and cook for 1 minute. Add tomatoes, wine, remaining pesto, and sugar. Bring to a boil, reduce heat, and simmer for 12–15 minutes; season with salt and pepper and reserve.
5. On a clean work surface, place cabbage leaf down. Trim the core. Place ½ cup mixture on top of each leaf. Fold sides in toward center and roll tightly. Repeat with remaining cabbage leaves and filling. Place rolls in a large oven-safe heavy casserole or sauté pan. Top with sauce. Bring to a boil on top of the stove, cover, and place in preheated oven for 1 hour. Uncover and cook for 15 minutes more or until tender.

STUFFING A CABBAGE LEAF

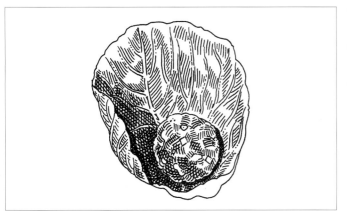

1. Put about half a cup of filling near the base of the leaf.

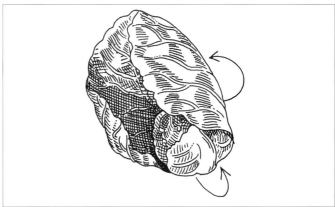

2. Fold the sides in toward the center.

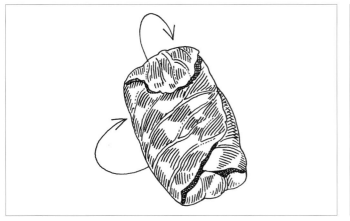

3. Roll up tightly.

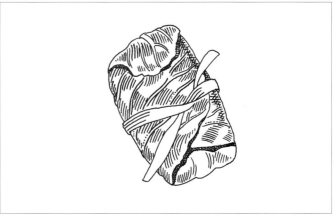

4. Just before serving, tie cabbage with a strip of leek that has been blanched and cooled.

PEAR AND RASPBERRY COBBLER

SERVES 6

We used Bosc pears for this recipe with superb results!

- 2 pounds pears, peeled and sliced (approximately 5 medium)
- 2 cups raspberries, fresh or frozen
- 1 cup plus 2 tablespoons flour
- ¼ cup granulated sugar
- ½ teaspoon ground cinnamon
- 1 stick unsalted margarine

1. Preheat oven to 350°F.

2. In a medium bowl toss together pears, raspberries, 2 tablespoons flour, and ¼ cup granulated sugar. Place in a 2-quart shallow casserole dish.

3. In a medium bowl combine remaining ingredients. Cut margarine with pastry blender until mixture resembles coarse meal. Spread liberally over pear-and-raspberry mixture. Bake for 40–45 minutes until fruit mixture begins to bubble.

The menorah should be kindled near a window, so its light can also illuminate the world outside. Each night an additional candle is added to teach us that we should always increase our efforts to spread light and goodness everywhere.

CHANUKAH

CANDLES IN THE WINDOW. Light in a dark place. The powerful glow of precious hope and a much needed miracle. It is no wonder that lighting the menorah is such a very special moment for children and adults alike. ✳ The festival, which begins on the twenty-ninth of Kislev, commemorates the victory of the tiny Maccabee army over the Syrian-Greek superpower that controlled Israel in the second century B.C.E.. It's interesting to consider that the Greeks were actually fond of the Torah. They appreciated the beauty and wisdom of its literature, ethics, and philosophy but rejected other aspects that were at odds with their practices. Particularly disdainful to the Greeks was the fact that the Torah mandated a day of rest for even the lowliest of workers and espoused a belief in only one God for all of humanity. ✳ Many Jews took Greek names, bowed to Greek idols, even dressed as they did. In fact, many of them rose to power and privilege by finally rejecting their own faith. Others, leaving behind their homes and possessions, ran off to the rural areas to escape Greek influence. When the Greek leader Antiochus moved to eliminate Jewish practices, Jewish leader Mattathias and his five sons, among them Judah the Maccabee, led a tiny army against the mighty in a struggle that culminated three years later. In 165 B.C.E., the Jews recaptured Jerusalem. Their first task was to cleanse and rededicate the Holy Temple and rekindle the Great Menorah, which was kept burning in the Temple at all times. The Talmud tells us that the Maccabees found only one flask of undefiled oil—enough to rekindle the Great Menorah for just one day. When the oil lasted for eight days, the exact amount of time needed for fresh oil to be pressed, it was clear that a miracle had taken place. ✳ Jews note the miracle of the oil with foods cooked in oil—potato latkes, doughnuts—and with the lighting of the eight-branched menorah. Although Chanukah's eight days can be a dazzling montage of parties, dreidels, latkes, and presents, its true essence is revealed in a single moment—the lighting of the menorah. When the candles are kindled, a beautiful flame composed of fire, wick, and oil bursts forth, a symbol of the goodness of Judaism, which has always shone forth to illuminate the world for us, our children, and everyone.

MENORAHS

This is the year to create an honest-to-goodness heirloom. If you're handy and brave, you can make a menorah like the one we've shown, to pass down through the generations. It's an intensely personal symbol of your faith, made from copper and steel. Once you master the technique, your design can be curvy or soft, contemporary and clear—whatever you choose. You might want to design some for special friends or family.

All the materials were purchased from a New York shop specializing in supplies to the costume jewelry trade. The hardest part of this project is learning how to solder, using a small blowtorch. But don't panic—chefs even use blowtorches to caramelize sugar as a finishing touch on pastry, and they're not welders! It does take some practice to get the hang of handling your materials, but you'll get the feel of it if you take your time. Don't rush this project. This method, learned well, can result in many beautiful treasures in the future, including jewelry, napkin rings, even dramatic lighting fixtures, all designed and created by you.

Get the family involved by creating the design together. If you're really a designer and not a craftsman, see if a local jeweler, sculptor, or shop will put together your menorah from your plans.

LIST OF MATERIALS

HANDHELD BUTANE TORCH

BENCH PIN

SPRING TWEEZERS

SILVER WIRE SOLDER

FLUX

4 MM. COPPER WIRE

3 MM. NICKEL-PLATED WIRE

COPPER CAPS

12" × 12" SOLDERING BLOCK

WIRE SNIPPERS

ROUND-NOSE PLIERS

EXTRA BUTANE

SMALL METAL SHOP FILE

SMALL WIRE BRUSH

*For extra help see
The Complete Metalsmith,
by Tim McCreight
(Davis Publications, 1982).

Give yourself some uninterrupted time to work with these tools. Work flat on your soldering block until all the pieces are ready to be assembled. Remember, the flux is the "glue" that holds together the pieces of metal, so use the flux whenever you solder a joint.

1. Do the menorah base first. Solder together two of the three center "feet" that make up the base supports. These pieces are made of the nickel-plated wire, and ours are about 12" long.

2. Next, make the circular base from the copper wire. It should measure about 6" in diameter. Of course, you can alter these plans as you go to make a larger or smaller finished piece. Just remember to adjust all pieces accordingly.

3. Working *flat* on your soldering block, using wire snippers, cut the pieces from copper wire that will form the arms that hold each candle cup. Cut each piece at least 2" longer than you need, because you can trim them off later. A rule of thumb: You can always remove a piece, but you can't add to a cut piece.

4. Using the round-nose pliers, shape each of the curves for the arms of your menorah. We used a baseball bat to bend the wire.

5. Solder the eight arms of your candleholders to the main upright support piece.

6. Now add your third "leg" for the center, about 18" long. This will be your main upright support piece and the longest upright in your menorah.

7. Join the bottoms of your three "legs" to the bottom circle base by soldering.

8. Using your wire snippers, trim off all the upright ends so that they are all the same height. They need to be straight so that when the candle cups are added, the eight arms will be uniform. Use a metal file to smooth the ends.

9. Turn the piece upside-down on the soldering block to join the eight copper cups to the eight arms of your menorah.

10. After you've finished the last nine steps, dunk your menorah into a sinkful of hot (not boiling) water for about 1 hour to soak away the flux.

11. The next day, use your wire brush to burnish your piece. Just brush all over to achieve a uniform glow. It really works, and the brushed metal looks wonderful.

12. If you like, try adding beads, glass drops, or interesting charms with head pins—available at the craft store in the jewelry section. An heirloom is created!*

VARIATIONS ON THE MENORAH

The tranquil rock menorah (*right*) is understated, elegant, almost Oriental in its classic simplicity. We used a beautiful tray and added natural polished river rocks around the candles for a distinctively different take on the traditional menorah. Just remember to place your *shamash*, or "helper," candle on a different level—higher works best for this style. Take an extra tea light, turn it upside-down, and mount the *shamash* on top. Hold it in place with a drop of hot wax. A simple, no-tools-needed object of beauty to light your holiday.

The olive oil menorah (*below*) is made simply of shot glasses. The secret to our oil menorah? Floating wicks, available at your local Judaica shop. We filled eight handsome shot glasses with

colored water, topped with an eighth inch of olive oil and a floating wick. For the *shamash*, use a standard candle, since it must light the oil. If you can, keep your menorah in a front window or doorway for passersby to see. Chanukah candles, according to Jewish law, should burn for at least thirty minutes, and candles should be set in a straight row, with the *shamash* higher than the rest of the candles.

Make a unique outside doorstep menorah (*not pictured*) with punched-pattern party bags. Nestle your candles inside glass tumblers and pop into the bag. If you choose to put a few inches of sand or cat litter inside the bag for anchoring purposes, sink the tumblers right into the sand for extra stability.

Everyone in the family should have a personal menorah. And just as families come in all ages, shapes, and sizes, so do menorahs. While most families prefer using candles, others have rediscovered olive oil, the precious fluid that led to our celebration of the miracle of Chanukah. We've shown a few menorah variations for you to consider, all made with a minimum of fuss from easily found materials.

Alphabet blocks create a bright, happy look for children, and a child's name may be substituted for the word "Chanukah." This is a great idea for families with more than one child—no fighting over whose menorah belongs to whom. Between Chanukahs each year, this menorah is a nice accent for a child's room. The materials come straight from the toy store. Choose your letter blocks, and pick up some fat, colorful wood balls for the feet and candleholders. Be sure to use standard wood glue for this project. It will make your menorah sturdier and long lasting. Mount and glue the blocks to a piece of wood from the hobby store. (Try the lumberyard's scrap pile first—they'll be happy to give you the wood you need at no charge.)

Paint your base a bright color to match one of the blocks. For the candleholders, insert small metal candle cups into the wood ball holes, and tap into the ball with a hammer. We've listed a source in the back of the book for these metal candle cups, which are specially fitted to hold standard Chanukah candles. Give the finished piece a quick spray of clear vanish, glue some felt circles to the bottom wood balls as table protectors, and you're finished. This is a wonderful baby gift, so keep it in mind throughout the year.

BEESWAX CANDLES

Nature's nod to the Festival of Lights, fragrant, freshly scented bundles of beeswax are a luxurious roll-your-own treat that make extra-special gifts, too. These are so simple to do that the children can get into the act and have instant success. Remember, you'll need a total of forty-four candles to cover the entire eight days of Chanukah, since you add a candle for each night and always use a "helper" candle, or *shamash*, to light the others. Beeswax comes in manageable sheets at the craft store, and a spool of waxed or unwaxed wicking is very inexpensive. In many ways, beeswax candles are more adaptable to different sorts of menorahs, since they're fairly easy to pinch and shape at the bottom, unlike the boxed Chanukah candles that are sold everywhere.

Beeswax sheets are available in loads of colors, but we stuck to a few neutral colors to show you a different look from the usual multicolored standbys. Make bundles for lucky friends, because beeswax candles in the gift shops are unbelievably pricey, and yours will cost a mere fraction of the price. Use a special ribbon to wrap the bundle of candles, and pack in a clear cellophane gift bag or natural woven basket.

Good news—you don't need much equipment to make a bountiful batch of beeswax candles, and it's not a messy job, either. We suggest that you pick up a rubber cutting mat at the art supply store. It's an investment, really, and you'll find yourself using the mat for many projects, some of which are in this book.

The mat protects your work surface and holds your work snug and slipproof, and they're marked with a grid to help make cut edges straight.

Unpack your menorahs and decide which wax colors will work best, then head out to the craft store. Do a little arithmetic to see how many sheets you'll need for each menorah, and buy accordingly. Multiply your 5½ inches of wicking for each candle by 44 to get a Chanukah's worth of wicking for your candles (22 feet should do it).

After your wax and wicks are all cut, the fun begins. Rolling is simple, quick, and clean, and it won't take long to amass quite a pile. The aroma is wonderful—like honey and fresh air. It's a perfect time to tell the little ones how bees are responsible for this pure, beautiful product as they roll. Remember to keep a gentle yet constant pressure on the wax as you roll, count forty-four candles for each menorah, and have a wonderful time with this project to be proud of.

BEEWAX CANDLES STEP-BY-STEP

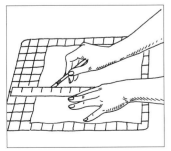

1. Using an X-Acto knife and straight-edge ruler, cut wax sheets into 2" × 4½" rectangles.

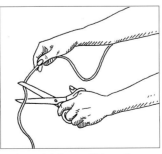

2. Cut wick into 5½" lengths.

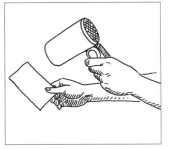

3. Warm wax with a hair dryer, if needed, until just a little soft.

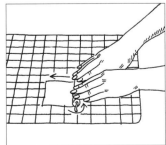

4. Place the wicking about ½" from one edge of the wax. Roll wax gently but firmly, sealing the final edge smooth lengthwise.

GELT BAGS

The giving of gelt, updated. Pretty parcels with panache, made of shimmering, gauzy organza, are a special treat for the children in your life, and they're as simple to make as sewing a straight line. Although toys, puzzles, and games have replaced Chanukah gelt in many communities, the fifth night of the festival is still regarded as a gelt-giving night, right after lighting the menorah. Traditional gelt bags were made of velvet, but today, anything goes. Ours are sewn from silvery see-through organza that gives children a glimpse of their gelt treats inside. Each bag has a surprise that teaches a lesson—a matching minibag to encourage children to give 10 percent of their windfall to charity, modeled on the tradition that 10 percent of one's income is to go to charity. You can help them deliver the bags to the organization of their choice—the synagogue, a soup kitchen, or children's hospital or shelter.

Organza comes in lots of lush colors, but we chose silver in honor of Chanukah. With pinking shears, cut two rectangles for each large bag, about 4 inches by 7 inches. After pinning the two pieces together, stitch across the bottom and up both sides. Turn the bag inside out for a finished look, instantly. Use the same method for the minibags, using rectangles about 2½ inches by 4 inches. Place rolled bills and coins in the bags, and tie with silver cord or pretty ribbons form your favorite fabric store. Finish off with silky tassels.

This can be a really sophisticated look, so you might consider some tabletop artistry for your Chanukah dinner party, using the same silvery organza. For a centerpiece, bag a crystal vase with the fabric, and tie with the same silver cord and a trio of tassels. Fill the vase with sprayed silver pods, branches, and foliage, and tie matching minibags onto the branches. For each place setting, present each guest with a large and small gelt bag. In the large bag, tuck in a scroll containing famed twelfth-century scholar Maimonides' Eight Degrees of Charity and a list of appropriate organizations that would benefit from some grown-up gelt on Chanukah. Fill the bag with silver chocolate coins.

THE EIGHT DEGREES OF CHARITY

1. The lowest degree is when one gives grudgingly.

2. Next in degree is when one gives less than he should, but gives graciously.

3. Better than the last is one who gives only after he has been asked.

4. Even better would be the person who gives before he has been asked.

5. Next best is when the poor knows from whom he receives, but the giver does not know to whom he gives.

6. The next degree is when the giver knows to whom he gives but the poor does not know from whom he receives.

7. Almost best is to give charity to the poor, but not know to whom he gives, and the poor man does not know whom it is from.

8. And the highest degree is to take hold of a person who has been crushed and to give him a gift or a loan, or to enter into partnership with him, or to find work for him, and thus put him on his feet so that he will not be dependent on his fellow man.

—Moses Maimonides

Gelt bags shimmer in the
winter sunlight, waiting for
Chanukah to begin.

GIFT WRAP

It's a wrap. While in the past children usually just received gelt, or money gifts, for Chanukah, many parents today also give gifts. Here, we've shown some interesting and beautiful ways to wrap all your gifts for the Festival of Lights.

So make a pot of coffee, clear off your worktable, and steal some time to create handmade Chanukah gift wrappings that are every bit as special as the gifts inside—with beaded ribbons, stamped papers, add-on enhancements that dangle dramatically or shimmer like the moon, including buttons and shiny silver or gold foil-wrapped chocolate gelt. We've wrapped up our treasures in silvers and blues, but the colors are really up to you.

Clockwise from top right: Glitzy metallic blue paper is all tied up with a swath of wide, sheer ribbon with gold-beaded edges. The bow is accessorized with a gold dreidel and tied on with slender metallic thread, available by the spool in sewing stores. (Hint: If you cannot find metallic dreidels, simply spread a handful of the very inexpensive dreidels on a sheet of newspaper and spray them with metallic paint. The multicolored plastic dreidels can be bought from Judaica stores in bags of one hundred, in several sizes to suit your needs.)

Silver on silver is a magical look, and it's easy to complete the look with punched-tin ornament tie-ons with personalized letter accents. Buy some disposable foil pie or roasting pans at your local dollar store, use a cookie cutter to trace your design, and cut it out with regular household scissors. Freehand or trace the initial for the center

(stencils work well), and carefully cut out the letter with a sharp X-Acto knife. Use a paper hole puncher to make the hole for the ribbon to slip through. Tie the ribbon onto the package bow, and you're finished. We used a Star of David, but just about any shape will work. Do an entire batch at a time.

We put our favorite silver metallic pens to work again, and this time for doodled gift wrap that looks professional no matter what. Use names, Chanukah symbols, dots, squiggles, and stars to create your very own look. Ours was done on blue paper and loaded up with a terrific topping of curled ribbons.

Wrap irregular shapes in fabric, for the flexibility that paper can't provide. This light-as-air metallic is gathered at the top, and the edges are cut with pinking shears. The cording, used for pillows, draperies, and upholstery, is a beautiful tie-up. Link a hand-

ful of shiny metal buttons with metallic thread for a knockout accent.

The tiny Stars of David on the gift wrap and satiny bow are really from bags of bar mitzvah confetti, sold in card and party stores by the bag. On newspaper, lay out a constellation of these stars, then spray with artists' spray mount so that they're sticky on one side and ready to affix to your wrapped and beribboned gifts.

The blue box is papered with metallic blue, then dotted with randomly placed silver pen marks. The package gets all dressed up with sheer, pretty ribbon and a cluster of shiny foil-covered chocolate Chanukah coins, or gelt. To make holes in the coins, place on a wooden board, run a skewer through the coin, and use a metallic thread to tie the coins onto the bow.

These wrap-ups only look difficult, and they're bound to be received with compliments and delight.

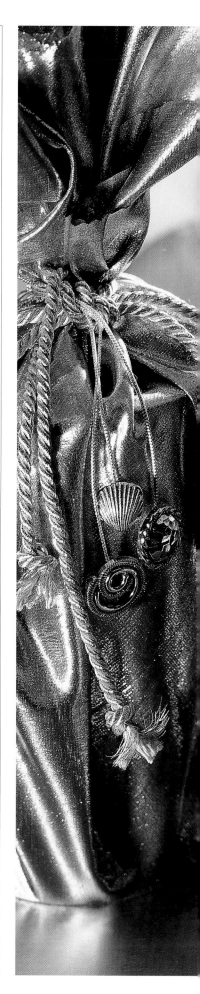

COOKIES

Cookies speak a special language. They tell of extra effort and time spent to delight guests of every age, every taste. Crisp and thin, yielding and chewy, cookies are the original ice-breakers—inviting comparison, eliciting admiration, and prompting nostalgic memories of other special times long past.

Visually, a cookie tray is a vivid still-life, a mélange of sweetness bursting with color, texture, and shape. Irresistibly tactile and easy to handle, they're a tempting, witty conclusion to your Chanukah buffet or open house. Children love to help with cookie rolling, cutting, and shaping, and they're pros with original decoration ideas, too. Buy a handful of Chanukah cookie cutters at your local kitchen shop and try your hand at a cookie tray. Try one kind at a time. Cookies store well, and soon you'll have a wonderful variety of sweets to offer your guests. An added bonus for you—a house smelling wonderfully of baking cookies is like taking a minivacation away from the pressures of everyday life.

COOKIE TIPS

• Use flat, no-side cookie sheets to ensure nice, even baking.
• Underbake rather than overbake cookies, by a minute or two. Too much time makes colored doughs too dark around the edges.
• Allow cookies to cool completely and to "set up" before storing.
• Use an airtight container to store your cookies. You may freeze them in a plastic container if you're baking way ahead.
• Try "painting" your plain cookies for a lovely stained-glass look. Mix an egg yolk with a few drops of food coloring for each hue, and before baking, paint cookie surfaces. Use an inexpensive artist's brush and rinse with water between colors.

Consider color, shape, taste, and size when you plan your cookie assortment. Even if you plan to use the same basic dough for several varieties, make sure they look as different as possible, with the use of icings, sugars, and colored decorations.

We choose simple yet beautifully complementary cookies for our tray. On the bottom, our stars are really white-and dark-chocolate-covered pretzels, made from thin pretzel sticks. Dip each stick into melted chocolate, form a Jewish star on waxed paper, and allow to dry. Use sprinkles before the chocolate dries.

Our glittery Stars of David are basic sugar cookies with blue-tinted sugar and piped-on white icing borders. Behind the stars, a chocolate lover's treat—apricots dunked in dark, sweet chocolate.

On the middle tier, rich and buttery marzipan dreidel cookies that look like the real thing. They take a bit of time to shape, but they're worth the effort, as you can see. To the right, giant dreidel sugar cookies are frosted with royal icing and dotted with blue icing for contrast. And on the left, six-pointed stars wear drizzles of chocolate that add simple stripes in seconds. On the top, tiny shortbread cookie coins resemble traditional gelt. We've stacked them and wrapped them in cellophane coin rolls tied up with ribbons on each end.

The choices are many, and it's up to you. We've given you a sampling of our favorites, but we're sure you have favorites that will make a wonderful cookie tray.

The cookie tray: a hands-on way to wish your guests a Happy Chanukah. Here, a half-dozen sweet ideas to tempt every guest at your Chanukah get-together.

LATKES

The sizzle of Chanukah begins and ends with potato latkes. And a word to the wise: Make lots. You'll need every last one of these crisp, crunchy classics that conjure up warm memories of past Chanukahs. Although many cultures offer a variation on the potato pancake, the Jewish version is undisputed king of the potato hill.

Because latkes are the main attraction at a Chanukah meal, and because latkes-in-progress need close watching, you don't need elaborate accompaniments. Make a mammoth fresh fruit salad earlier in the day and a triple batch of tart and creamy coleslaw for texture and contrast, pick up some fresh challah rolls at the bakery, and set out big bowls of applesauce and sour cream.

We offer three versions for you to try. For the purist, the classic potato latke, made simply of grated potatoes, onions, eggs, and matzo meal. (No, you cannot use flour instead of matzo meal for authentic latkes!) Sweet-potato latkes are more moist than the classic and use dark brown sugar and pumpkin pie spices to bump up the flavor nicely. And for the nouveau adventurist, our root vegetable latkes are a must-try.

To get the best latkes possible, most experts suggest using a heavy cast-iron skillet. Iron distributes even heat for consistent frying, and the skillet will last for decades. You must "season" the skillet before using, according to manufacturer's instructions. It takes a while, but the results are worth it.

A word about potatoes—don't get fancy. The best potatoes for superb latkes are the no-frills, all-purpose potatoes like Idaho or russet. Just give them a good scrubbing to clean them up before peeling or grating.

For the lazy at heart, leave on the potato skins. Once you try these, you'll probably never peel potatoes for latkes again.

Use any kind of oil you like. Your doctor might be pleased to know that canola oil, one of the heart-healthier oils, makes a luscious latke, but combinations of other oils are very good, too.

Throw away your first latke. Our theory is that if you heat up your oil gradually, using the sample pancake as a thermometer, it is better than taking the chance of getting splattered with hot oil.

For large batches, plan to change your oil at least once or twice. Oil can become dirty on the bottom of the pan, turn black, and start to smoke, and adding more oil won't remedy the situation. It's better to keep the oil pure and clean for consistently delicious latkes.

Drain your latkes on paper shopping bags. Cut down the side of the bag to the bottom, flatten out the paper, turn inside out to avoid any printing on the front, fold double, and drain your latkes. It keeps the pancakes crisper than paper towels do.

Last, keep your finished latkes warm in a 300°F oven, uncovered, until you're ready to serve.

Stay with the classics, or try new versions, like these root vegetable latkes.

CLASSIC POTATO LATKES

MAKES 18 PANCAKES

2 pounds russet potatoes (8 medium potatoes), peeled
1 medium yellow onion
2 large eggs, beaten
½ cup matzo meal
2 teaspoons kosher salt
½ teaspoon cracked black pepper
Vegetable oil for frying

1. Grate potatoes and onions in a food processor, using the shredding blade. Remove mixture to a bowl and replace shredding blade with steel blade. In batches, pulse-process the potato mixture for 10–15 seconds. Place mixture in a strainer over a bowl, and squeeze out extra liquid. (Reserve liquid. Wait 2–3 minutes—water will separate from the starch by rising to the top and the starch will be on the bottom of the bowl. Pour water out and use starch in step 2.)

2. Place strained potatoes in a medium-size bowl. Fold in eggs, matzo meal, salt, pepper, and reserved potato starch. Mix well.

3. In a cast-iron skillet over medium heat, heat vegetable oil. Oil should be about 1 inch deep.

4. Form ¼ cup potato mixture into pancakes and slide gently into oil. Let cook for 6–8 minutes or until golden on one side. Flip pancakes and continue cooking for 6–8 minutes. Drain pancakes on paper towels and serve immediately.

SUGGESTIONS

• Latkes can be portioned with an ice-cream scoop and then flattened out when they are in the pan.

• These make large latkes, but this batter is perfect for mini–potato latkes, too.

• Latkes freeze beautifully. Cook according to recipes, cool, and freeze. Reheat at 400°F for 10–12 minutes or until heated through.

SWEET-POTATO LATKES

MAKES 16 PANCAKES

2 large eggs, beaten
1 tablespoon dark brown sugar
1 teaspoon apple pie spice
1 teaspoon kosher salt
½ teaspoon black pepper
4½ cups shredded sweet potatoes (approximately 2 large potatoes)
½ cup matzo meal
Vegetable oil for frying

1. In a food processor fitted with a steel blade, puree eggs, brown sugar, apple pie spice, salt, and pepper until smooth. Add 2 cups shredded sweet potatoes and matzo meal, and pulse-puree for 15–20 seconds.

2. Transfer mixture to a medium-size bowl. Stir in remaining sweet potatoes.

3. In a large cast-iron skillet over medium-high heat, heat vegetable oil. Oil should be about 1 inch deep.

4. Form ¼ cup potato mixture into pancakes and slide gently into oil. Let cook for 6–8 minutes or until golden on one side. Flip pancakes and continue cooking for 6-8 minutes or until golden. Drain pancakes on paper towels or paper shopping bags and serve immediately.

ROOT VEGETABLE LATKES

MAKES 18 PANCAKES

1 cup shredded carrot (1 medium)
1 cup shredded celeriac (1 medium)
1 cup shredded parsnip (1 medium)
¼ cup shredded leek (1 medium, trimmed and rinsed)
1¼ cups shredded beets, rinsed and drained well (1 large)
2 cups shredded Idaho or russet potatoes
2 large eggs, beaten
½ cup matzo meal
2 teaspoons kosher salt
½ teaspoon cracked black pepper
Vegetable oil for frying

1. In a large bowl combine carrots, celeriac, parsnip, leek, and beets; reserve.

2. In a food processor fitted with the steel "S" blade, pulse-process potatoes for 30 seconds. Add to shredded vegetables along with eggs, matzo meal, salt, and pepper. Mix well.

3. In a large cast-iron skillet, over medium-high heat, heat vegetable oil. Oil should be about 1 inch deep.

4. Form ¼ cup potato mixture into pancakes and gently slide into oil. Let cook for 6–8 minutes or until golden on one side. Flip pancakes and continue cooking for 6–8 minutes or until golden. Drain pancakes on paper towels or paper shopping bags and serve immediately.

BASIC SUGAR COOKIES

MAKES ABOUT 4 DOZEN

¼ cup butter or margarine
1 cup sugar
2 eggs
1 teaspoon vanilla extract
2½ cups flour
1 teaspoon baking powder
1 teaspoon salt

1. Cream the butter and sugar together until the mixture is light yellow in color.

2. Add the eggs and vanilla.

3. Blend in the flour, baking powder, and salt. Cover and chill for 1 hour.

4. Preheat oven to 400°F. On a lightly floured board, roll out the dough, thin if you like crisp cookies or thicker if you prefer them soft.

5. Cut out the desired shapes with cookie cutters. Lift cookies with a spatula onto an ungreased cookie sheet.

6. Bake for about 6–8 minutes or until very light brown.

VARIATIONS

• Icing can be made to decorate cookies by mixing one box (1 pound) of confectioners' sugar with 5 tablespoons meringue powder and ½ cup water.

• Tiny "gelt cookies" are made using a soda bottle top as a cookie cutter.

• Chocolate chunks can be placed in a resealable plastic bag, and microwaved until chocolate melts, about one minute. Snip a very small hole in a corner of bag and drizzle chocolate over cookies in stripes or desired patterns.

MARZIPAN DREIDEL COOKIES

MAKES ABOUT 2 DOZEN

½ **cup butter or margarine, softened**
¼ **cup sugar**
1¼ **cups flour**
Food coloring

1. Preheat oven to 300°F.
2. Cream the sugar and butter together.
2. Add flour and mix well.
3. Divide into 3 or 4 equal parts, adding different-colored food coloring to each part.
4. Form the dreidel shapes by hand and using a straight edge like a knife. To form the "top," use a wood skewer, cut into short pieces, and cover with colored dough.
5. Chill cookies for at least 30 minutes.
6. Bake for about 25 minutes.

CHOCOLATE PRETZEL STARS

There's no baking required for these fun treats.
Let the kids help with this one.

6 **ounces semisweet chocolate**
1 **tablespoon vegetable shortening**
Pretzel sticks

1. In a medium saucepan, melt chocolate over low heat. Stir in shortening.
2. Let cool for a few minutes.
3. Stir in the pretzel sticks until well coated with chocolate. Arrange on waxed paper sheets, forming six-pointed stars. If desired, sprinkle with colored sugar or tiny colored nonpareils.
4. Chill for about 1 hour.

SHORTBREAD COOKIES

MAKES ABOUT 2 DOZEN

These melt-in-your-mouth cookies are best kept in small shapes since they are very rich.

¼ **cup butter or margarine, softened**
¼ **cup sugar**
2 **cups flour**

1. Preheat oven to 350°F.
2. Cream the butter and sugar.
3. Add flour and mix well.
4. Roll out dough about ⅓ inch thick on a lightly floured board. Cut into shapes and place 1 inch apart on an ungreased cookie sheet. Bake for 20 minutes. Let cool.

Paper Dreidel Template

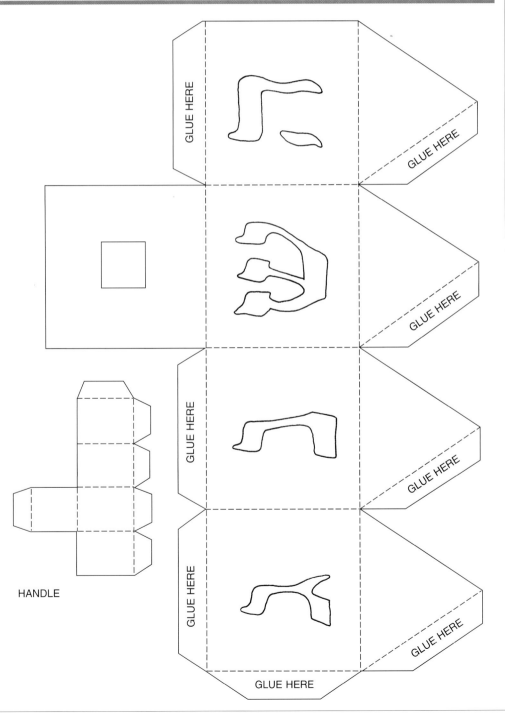

HANDLE

PAPER DREIDELS

We have lots of uses for these charming, fun-to-make paper dreidels. They don't spin fast enough to use for the dreidel game, but you can use them as party favors, filled with candy. Try them as place cards at your annual Chanukah latke party. Tuck a present inside for a truly unique gift box. String them like paper lanterns on yarn or ribbon (or even along a string of blue miniature lights) across the room or around the front door of your home. With lighted menorahs in your front windows and dreidels on your door, you might want to take a nighttime photo for next year's Chanukah cards.

At any rate, these oversize dreidels are a festive, fun symbol of the season, and they're simple to make, using our pattern. A copy machine helps make the size you need, and it's a great project for the entire family. Use heavyweight paper or card stock to help your dreidels hold their shape and to make them strong enough to hold candy, favors, or gifts. Be wild and crazy with your colors—don't stick just to blue and white!

Use the template on page 67 as a basic design for your own dreidels. Remember, a copy machine can make them just the sizes you need and reproduce them on just the heavyweight paper color(s) you want. For size, using the copier at 145 percent enlargement will fit on an 8½-by-11-inch sheet of paper. For big, big sizes, Kinko's can run them on heavyweight card stock on their poster-size copier, and you can get up to 24-by-28-inch patterns for a real statement!

1. Carefully cut out all the shapes indicated by solid lines only; use scissors for regular cuts and your X-Acto knife for hard-to-reach cuts.

2. Color in the Hebrew letters with acrylic paints for a festive colorful look, or outline in paint pens. Or you can trace the letters onto colored paper, then cut out and paste in position.

3. Next, score on the dotted lines by lightly running the X-Acto knife against a metal ruler along those dotted lines to score the paper for easier, cleaner folding. Remember, a light touch—you don't want to cut all the way through the paper.

4. Try rubber cement as an adhesive. Apply on all the "glue here" areas on the pattern. Carefully bend all pieces on the body of the dreidel into place, then press down the glued flaps, forming the sides first.

5. When the sides are glued together, it's time for the bottom. Glue the flaps on the bottom and fold carefully, forming the point. Leave the top unglued.

6. If you would like to hang your dreidel from a string (as pictured), be sure to punch a starter hole, using a skewer, in the top of the handle while it is still flat. Pull a string through the hole. Knot the end, so the string doesn't slip through the hole. Now, glue the flaps on the tiny handle and paste into the top lid.

7. Last, glue the top lid where indicated and close up carefully.

Ness Gadol Hayah Sham— a great miracle happened there.
—2,300-YEAR-OLD ACRONYM OF TRADITIONAL DREIDEL TOY

Our paper dreidels have many uses, from hanging decorations to place cards to party favors.

The most widespread custom for the celebration of Tu B'Shvat
is the enjoyment of many different fruits. Many observe
this holiday by eating fifteen different types, since the holiday
falls on the fifteenth of the month.

TU B'SHVAT

CHERISHED SINCE ANCIENT TIMES, TREES ARE A SYMBOL of strength and beauty. And to Jews, trees are also a symbol of birth and life. In ancient Israel it was a custom for parents to plant a tree when a baby boy or girl was born—cedar for boys, cypress for girls. When the children were ready to marry, the branches of their trees were entwined to build their marriage canopy, or *huppah*. ✳ Every year, to celebrate the Jewish people's special relationship with trees, Tu B'Shvat, the original Arbor Day, is celebrated on the fifteenth of the Hebrew month of Shevat. It is about this time that the fruit trees are blossoming in Israel. The Jewish people always considered fruit trees, in particular, to be a special kindness from God. While there are many foods that will sustain us, the fruit tree gives us more than mere sustenance—from their graceful branches come shade, wonderful fragrance, and an almost endless variety of luscious fruits. ✳ In 70 C.E. the Holy Temple in Jerusalem was destroyed, and the Jews went into exile all over the world. Since that time Jews have sought to reconnect and bind themselves to the land of Israel on Tu B'Shvat each year by eating fruits and nuts common there, such as dates, figs, grapes, olives, and pomegranates. In present-day Israel, Tu B'Shvat is marked by field trips and the planting of seedlings by schoolchildren. This special love for trees and the environment is not surprising, as our 3,300-plus-year-old Torah has detailed laws governing the care of the land long before the creation of the Environmental Protection Agency. ✳ Our sages have also loved trees for the lessons they teach. Just as a tree needs to have strong roots in the earth to survive and eventually go on to bear fruit, so too should a child be rooted in the beauty and wisdom of our tradition. ✳ In many ways, the timeless beauty of the tree and the tenacious strength of the Jews create a perfect spiritual marriage. Celebrate this spiritual marriage in your home during Tu B'Shvat as you wait out the final weeks of winter and prepare your inner self for the busy schedule of the season to come.

MINIATURE TREES

When Tu B'Shvat comes to Israel, the trees are in bud. In North America and in much of the Diaspora, the trees are bare, the weather frigid, and there may be a blanket of snow on the ground. Never mind. Bring the spirit of the holiday of trees to your corner of the world with a miniature tree, trimmed in a semitopiary fashion. While you're trimming your topiaries, start from scratch for next year: pop some citrus seeds into foam cups filled with vermiculite and keep them moist enough to sprout within two weeks. When your seedlings are up to a few inches, transfer them to small pots. Keep them watered and fertilized, and you'll have a mininursery of trees for next year's celebration of Tu B'Shvat, and enough to give to friends.

The world is a tree and human beings are its fruit.
—RABBI SOLOMON IBN GABIROL

There are two ways to go with our Tu B'Shvat trees. You may buy them, already trimmed, from your local florist, or you may trim them yourself. Have fun finding wonderful pots and creative soil toppers, keeping your special look in mind. Decide in which room you'd like your tree to "live," and pick your basic spot before you shop, keeping availability and direction of light in mind. We've given you three types to consider: foliage-only, a fruiting variety, and a lush flowering tree.

First and fabulous, the ficus. Found in virtually every greenhouse, home center, and florist, the ficus is a home-loving plant that has a preference for sunny windows and an occasional misting to remind it of its original home in the tropics. Keep the soil moist but not soggy, and let the surface soil dry between waterings. Try beautiful stones rather than moss for a distinctive look.

Fruit trees are fun to have at home, and just looking at a miniature orange tree (calamondin) might conjure up visions of Israel's Jaffa orange groves. This is a charming tree: its foliage is dark green and glossy, and tiny, fragrant white flowers precede the tiny edible oranges. Just keep the soil moist and feed every month except during the winter.

Azaleas are fabulous florals—from pristine whites, pale pinks, and lilacs to startling hot pinks and deep reds, azaleas are a magic show of color and, inside the home, a welcome spring preview. They love dappled sunlight and moist soil. When danger of frost has passed, plant them in the garden.

Winter wake-ups to celebrate Tu B'Shvat: a trio of tiny trees. *From left to right:* The handsome ficus; a miniature orange tree; an azalea topiary just beginning to flower.

FRUIT CENTERPIECES

The traditional Tu B'Shvat table displays three sorts of fruits for tasting, and so have we. Rather than ho-hum baskets displaying each type, we've created bouquets, trees, and topiaries made of fruit, and each process is less daunting than it looks.

Now, the three fruit types. These fruits are offered as a vital part of Tu B'Shvat observance so that we may note and appreciate their ingenious differences. The first group includes those that have a peel or shell and cannot be eaten without removing their outer coverings. Examples of these include bananas, oranges, kiwis, walnuts, and mangoes. The second group includes all fruits that are edible both inside and out, including grapes, apples, pears, strawberries, and figs. The third group are those with pits or seeds that cannot be eaten, such as apricots, olives, dates, plums, cherries, and kumquats.

Face it, these fanciful fruit masterpieces have an undeniably decorator look, and here's the good news: Not only are they quite simple to assemble, but by using your own fruit combinations and personal touches, you create your own signature look.

Fruit centerpieces celebrate the spirit of Tu B'Shvat in a vivid, knockout way. Our edible creations include, *Left:* A "bouquet" of mini bananas, kiwis, oranges, and mangoes and walnuts spilling out of your favorite vase like a bunch of exotic flora. *Center:* A foraged tree limb "grows" a fantasy feast of lady apples, Seckel pears, and fat strawberries. *Right:* Sleek, shiny, and symmetrical, our topiary only looks priceless. Black plums, kumquats, and olives march in uniform rows touched with edible greenery to create this elegant showstopper.

Beginning with the fruit bouquet at the far left, choose a container in the height you'd like, fill it with florist's foam, and gather the fruits you plan to use. Use inexpensive wooden skewers (they look like pickup sticks), and gently insert one end into each piece of fruit and the other securely into the foam. Stand back and use your critical eye as you build your bouquet, so that you get just the shape, overhang, and height that pleases you most.

For the fruit tree, scout the backyard for a fallen limb of the right proportion and place in a favorite container. Use a large florist's frog for support at the bottom to secure the branch, pack with green floral foam called "oasis," and top with moss or pebbles. Then hang your fruits from the branches with silky ribbons. Hot glue some silk leaves near the fruit stems for an unexpectedly natural look.

Our fruit topiary looks too pretty to eat, but since these are the fruits that are ready to eat, we've attached them to the Styrofoam cone with toothpicks so that your guests may help themselves. It looks tricky, but the key is this: Plan your color rows before you begin, and start from the top, always. By the time you get to the bottom near your container, you'll be a pro. Another trick is to fill bare spots with fresh curly parsley or, if you can find them, fragrant bunches of mint leaves.

The word "Purim" comes from the Hebrew word pur, *meaning lot or lottery, which is how the date for the destruction of the Jews was chosen.*

PURIM

UNCLE ABE IN A DRESS? The cantor impersonating a chicken? Of course—it's Purim, the definitive holiday of joy and merriment. The story of Purim has all the ingredients of an Emmy-winning soap opera—love, hate, desire, intrigue, beauty, and, yes, the beast. ✳ The drama goes something like this: During the seventy years between the First and Second Temples, the Jews were scattered throughout Persia. They were prosperous and well established, and some even found their way into the court of King Ahasuerus. When his wife, Vasti, refused to dance unclothed in front of his guests, she was killed and replaced by Esther, who kept her Jewish identity tightly under wraps. One of the king's advisers, Mordechai, was an uncle of Esther's and a righteous leader among the Jews. One of the king's henchmen, Haman, was a confirmed hater of Jews, and he particularly abhorred Mordechai, an old enemy. The trouble began when Mordechai refused to bow down to his old adversary. In his fury, Haman—through lies and slanderous propaganda—convinced the king to sign a decree that the Jews of the kingdom would be destroyed. The date, the thirteenth of Adar, was chosen by a *pur,* or lottery. A special scaffold was built for Mordechai, but together, Mordechai and Esther overturned the evil decree against the Jews by appealing to God and by fasting for three days. The climax: a dinner party for two, where Esther wined and dined the king, revealed her Judaism, uncovered Haman's evil plot, and managed to have Haman hung from the very gallows built for Mordechai. ✳ This drama is recounted in the Megillah, in the Book of Esther, which is read each Purim. And although the Jewish people have faced many Hamans since the day of Ahasuerus, this chapter in our history gives us the strength to face them all and always to survive. ✳ On Purim we are so giddy with joy that we give ourselves up to merriment. Children and adults alike dress outrageously, in clever costume disguises that often take months of planning. There is noise, music, and dancing. Haman's name is drowned out during the Megillah reading with the harsh sounds of the graggers. Elaborate food gifts are sent to friends, and *tzedakah* is given to the poor. Never mind that it takes an average of three weeks to recover from one day of Purim. We celebrate for those who came before us, and we celebrate with our children so they may teach those who come after us.

SHALACH MANOT

This treasured Purim custom is more fun than a birthday party, and it lasts all day. Beautiful and creative food packages, both big and small, are delivered to Jewish families and friends in the neighborhood. In areas with large Jewish populations, the doorbell never stops ringing, and loads of change are kept by the door as "tips" for costumed children delivering *shalach manot* and for the giving of *tzedakah*, another mitzvah taken very seriously on Purim. In Hebrew, *shalach manot* means to "send out portions," and that's just what it is. Here's all you need to know: Include at least two items of ready-to-eat food or drink in your food basket. Although you are obligated to send a food gift to only one person, you'll get carried away and make a list of recipients, especially if you've developed a terrific theme.

We've shown a few of our favorites, but this is just the beginning. Try an Italian theme, packed in big colanders, or maybe an apple theme—real half-peck baskets filled with apple-flavored foods. The sky's the limit, so work your own brand of *shalach manot* magic.

The garden basket is one of our family favorites. Recipients don't need to be gardeners to appreciate its spring-is-coming charm. Use a clay flowerpot, ceramic bowl, or simple wood container, all of which will be used long after the Purim treats are gone. Fill two-thirds of the container with Styrofoam peanuts, wadded newspaper, or tissue, then fill with dried moss or dried green grass. Glue bright seed packets to tops of craft sticks, slip in a great-looking gardening hand tool, and fill with your choice of herbal teas, exotic juices, handsomely packaged jams, and crackers. Tuck in some hamantaschen, the traditional fruit-stuffed pastry shaped like the evil Haman's hat, add a homemade gift tag taped with a wood skewer, and add a fabric bow—plaid is special; checks are cheery yet subtle.

First-timers find that filling a Chinese takeout box is fun and easy to do. Buy the boxes from your favorite Chinese fast food, or pick up the shiny lacquered-look boxes in the party store. Fill with chopsticks, fortune cookies, rice vinegar, duck sauce, stir-fry oils, and a packet of loose green tea. Try red or black Mylar for the package filler or maybe some shredded Chinese newspaper, and wrap the entire package in wide clear cellophane.

Opposite page: **Use different pots and containers to create our shalach manot garden basket. Using the assembly-line method makes short work of filling, adding accents, and labeling gift baskets.** *This page:* **Stylish and crisp, the Chinese takeout box makes a major statement, filled to the brim with the makings of a Chinese feast.**

HAPPY PURIM!

FROM THE SHAPIRO FAMILY

Personalize Purim. There's a theme for everybody on your list, and everything's a potential container—just think of your recipients' special interests. Children? Plastic sand buckets, goldfish bowls, sombreros, bright-colored storage totes. For grown-ups, kitchen crocks for the cook. Tote bags for the day-tripper. A wine cooler for the entertainer. Big plastic popcorn bowls for armchair athletes. You get the idea.

Note what goes inside, too. For children, more small toys and portable snack foods, like pressed fruit sheets, juices, sugarless gum, and boxes of raisins. Seniors would appreciate more fruit and ready-baked goods. And a bachelor will thank you a thousand times for some home-cooked food. It is customary to tuck a small bottle of grape juice into each basket, so stock up when your stores have specials, no matter what time of year. And since a simple half mask looks festive threaded through your wrapping ribbon, stock up the day after Halloween.

Creative themes for *shalach manot* packages take much less work than you'd think. Our theme for the bedotted look on the left is "Things That Go Pop." Start thinking "pop" and you'll come up with lollypops, popcorn in some form, Pop-Tarts, bubble gum, champagne, or sparkling grape juice (the cork pops), bubble soap, and English crackers that pop when the end is pulled, spilling more goodies. We used inexpensive cardboard ice buckets from the party supply store, decorated with round yard sale stickers and colored with bright markers. Fill the buckets with shredded or wadded tissue paper, or try shiny Mylar. Add a mini Mylar balloon on a stick for your gift tag—we've sprayed ours hot pink, then added more sticker dots and the recipient's name and greeting.

On this page, our 100 percent natural basket makes a nice gift for your favorite Earth Week organizer, mountain climber, or lover of all things organic. Start with a twig basket and fill with straw or raffia (from the craft store).

Make a foray to the health food store and stock up on basket fillers that include trail mixes, bottled waters or natural juices, dried figs, apricots, or long papaya spears. Add a satisfying selection of whole-wheat crackers, carrot or pita chips, and a nice jug of pure maple syrup. Use textured, recycled paper or sturdy oak tag for your message and gift wrap.

If you've never tried the shrink-wrap trick, now's the time. Get a professionally finished look by draping your finished basket with this special cellophane wrap that is activated by your blow-dryer. Ask for it at your local craft store—it couldn't be easier to get a truly pro finish.

Design your Purim baskets with a personal touch. *Left:* **Tickle someone's funny bone with Things That Go Pop, or** *(right)* **put together a Purim basket that's truly a natural, loaded with treats from the natural foods store. Note that the** *halakah* **suggests that to fulfill the mitzvah of** *shalach manot*, **send at least two food gifts.**

COSTUMES

Purim carnivals are more fun than Mardi Gras. Crazier than Brazil's Carnival. And happier than Halloween could ever be. It's the ultimate let-your-hair-down Jewish hoedown, and many Jews consider it an obligation to drink schnapps until they can no longer remember the name of the enemy Haman.

But Purim brings out the best in kids and even the most jaded adults. In Jewish schools and community centers all over the country, Purim week is party week. Everyone dresses up, and in the synagogue, Cookie Monsters sit next to Raggedy Andys.

About costumes: The trick here is to win the costume parade, and that means a show of originality. Among the knee-high Queen Esthers, bad Hamans, and benign clowns, an offbeat original always shines through. A family of Japanese samurai and geishas, a gaggle of court jesters, and one year we spotted the entire cast of *The Wizard of Oz*. It makes you wonder: Is that really the Cowardly Lion over by the punch bowl, or is it the rabbi?

Enter our suggestions, beginning with the half-and-half family—being two-faced was never so clever! It's such a wonderful look, you might even carry the black-and-white theme right through to your *shalach manot* baskets. Decorate a white container with black dots or stripes and fill with black-and-white jelly beans, black-and-white iced cookies, black twist licorice sticks, and wrapped foods with black-and-white wrappers. Include some silver wrappers for added pizazz.

Walking, talking *shalach manot* treats. Delicious, different costumes for children, beginning with the candy button kid imitating the penny-candy crunchy dots on paper we loved when we were young. Candy is a good theme, and you can transform a toddler into a giant peppermint with a circle of foam core with painted stripes and a clear cellophane wrap. A bag of jelly beans is as simple as a clear plastic garbage bag filled with tiny balloons. Try copying the lettering on a real bag of jelly beans for a truly authentic touch.

Left: The two-faced how-to: Buy two pairs of sweatshirts and pants for each member of your troupe. Cut both the shirt and pants right down the middle of each, and sew together opposite halves. If you don't like to sew, a seamstress or tailor can do them easily. As for shoes, buy each person a pair of white sneakers and paint one black with shoe polish or acrylic paint. Pick up some black top hats from the party store, tape off half the hat down the middle, and spray the other half with white spray paint. For the faces, use clown or face paint, available everywhere.

Right: Button up the candy kid: Use two pieces of white tag or poster board, attached to each other with sturdy white duct tape that goes over the shoulders. Button candies are made of Styrofoam balls, cut in half and spray-painted with happy colors. Attach in rows with a glue gun. For the candy hat, hot glue a hair band to a Styrofoam ball.

Far right: For a *shalach manot* basket a child can really get into: Cut the bottom out of a discount store wicker hamper (we suggest using a pruning saw). Use two pieces of rope as shoulder straps. Decorate the basket with pretend fruit, big candy wrappers, a greeting tag, and a big homemade bow attached to the basket with floral wire.

GRAGGERS

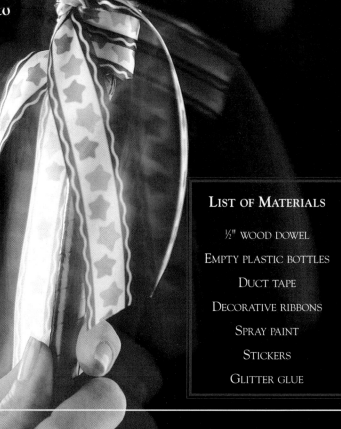

HAMAN! During the Megillah reading on Purim, the synagogue explodes into raucous noise whenever Haman's name is mentioned. Some rabbis use a police whistle to signal when to start and stop the noise, and one synagogue we know mounts a real traffic light on the *bimah*—with the green light to start the noise, red to cease.

A forerunner to modern graggers: In ancient times, children carved Haman's name on two sticks, and during the Megillah reading, they would hit the sticks together as hard as they could.

We've designed some very elegant graggers that are simple to make. They add a unique touch to all sorts of costumes, and they're safe enough for the smallest children since they have no sharp edges or holes for small fingers to get painfully stuck in—as the commercial metal noisemakers often do. These are ecologically correct, too—we've recycled used plastic soda, oil, and soap bottles for the rattle portions and filled them with dried beans. Here are just a few designs for you to get started on Purim's prettiest noisemakers.

Without a doubt, the most distinctive graggers at the Purim carnival. They are easy to make—give one a shake.

LIST OF MATERIALS

½" WOOD DOWEL

EMPTY PLASTIC BOTTLES

DUCT TAPE

DECORATIVE RIBBONS

SPRAY PAINT

STICKERS

GLITTER GLUE

Clean and dry your bottle thoroughly, then fill with dried beans. The first step in assembly is to insert the dowel into the bottle and secure it by tapping a small nail in one side of the bottle, through the dowel, and out the other side. Using duct tape, tape around the bottle top and down onto the wooden dowel for extra security. Paint the plastic bottle as you choose.

Opposite page: We used glossy black acrylic, then wrapped the dowel with black hockey tape before finishing with wrapped colored string, star stickers, and a length of starred ribbon.

Below left: Our silver gragger is a hand soap bottle sprayed with metallic paint and decorated with glitter glue designs. We wrapped the dowel in shiny silver ribbon and twisted a long silver star garland just under the rattle.

Below right: A lemon bottle needs no painting. The dots are stick-ons from the craft or card store, and the dowel handle received a coat of acrylic paint, then was sprayed with clear varnish. Gobs of curling ribbon tied around the top give this gragger a very festive look.

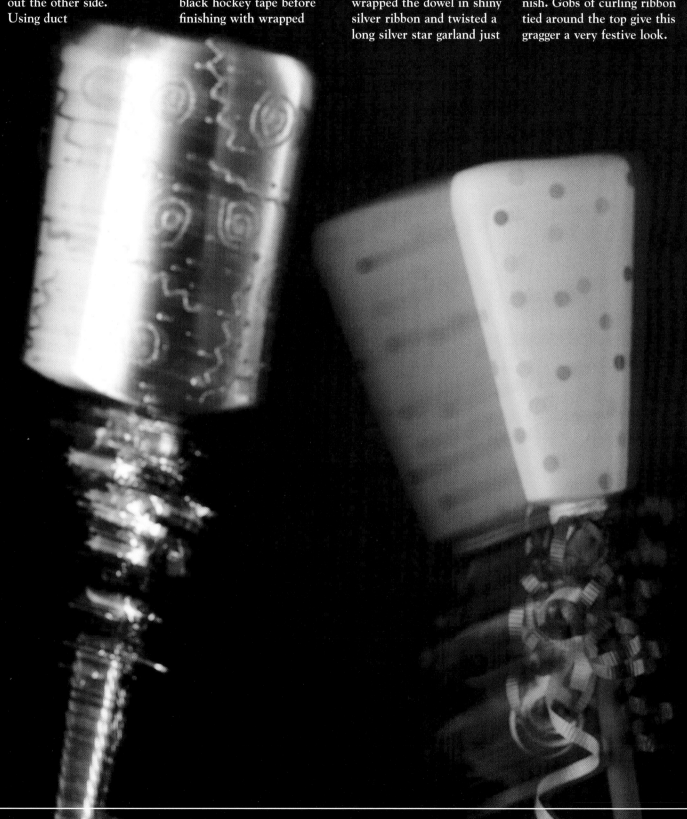

CHARITY BOXES

Purim is a wonderful time to get into the giving habit, because during this holiday we are required to give money gifts to at least two needy people or worthy causes. And even very young children take a special delight in pushing coins into charity boxes, thus ensuring that their earliest association with money will be that of helping others. Many homes have a kitchen windowsill crowded with charity, or *tzedakah*, boxes from Jewish schools and yeshivas, relief organizations, camps, orphanages, and synagogues. When you visit a kosher restaurant, you'll see a rainbow of *tzedakah* boxes, too.

Sometimes we as Jews are obligated to give, before Shabbat or a holiday—but at other times we want to give, to celebrate life's good news, such as a special birthday or a child's straight-A report card. Since giving is an intensely personal matter, your charity boxes should reflect your personal style as well. Go whimsical, cerebral, or nostalgic, but make sure it gives you pleasure to display it. And that way you'll be much more likely to use it often.

Give a face lift to the traditional cardboard-and-metal coin box your synagogue sends around, or use baking powder cans, cocoa tins, or tall potato crisp containers. Just cut a slot in the top to insert the coins.

Here, we've shown a few ideas to make a personal statement for your *tzedakah* boxes. Browse a craft or fabric store, and you'll come up with hundreds more.

For our benumbered box, we found stick-on numbers used for making creative clocks. After wrapping the box with a matte black paper, we scattered the self-sticking gold-toned numbers.

The photo can is one of our

Four fun ideas to inspire your own. *Clockwise from top left*: A montage of numbers, photo gallery, fun button display, and a simple but elegant corrugated cardboard cover.

favorites. Pick a favorite family photo, take it to the quick print center for a color copy, and glue it on. It's a good idea to take your container with you so that the copy machine operator can size it up or down accordingly. Cut the copy to fit the height of the can, wrap the image around the can, and secure with clear tape or spray the can with spray mount adhesive.

A way to use up those stray buttons—cover your can with felt or any colored paper and attach the buttons with a hot glue gun. We glued on a length of rickrack from the sewing store for a shot of silly pizzazz. A hint: Give this design to the children—they have great button and notion how-to.

A no-frills, knockout neutral look is as easy as having a

sheet of corrugated cardboard (always save from packing material) and some raffia for a pretty tie.

Use your imagination and have fun. Color copy the kids' artwork and create whimsical, colorful containers without sacrificing the original masterpieces. Wrap your *tzedakah* box in rope or fancy cording by using your glue gun and working your way down. Use tapestry fabric for an elegant look. Create a mosaic by using chunks of broken pottery, china, or tile. Encourage your family to get into the habit of giving. As each box becomes full, allow the children to take turns deciding where the money will go. Giving charity is one of humanity's most compassionate acts and one for which the Jewish people are well-known.

Charity lengthens one's days and years.
—TANA DEVE' ELIYAHU ZUTA

Purim pizzazz. Traditional
hamantaschen with nouveau
fillings for you to try: elegant
pecan raspberry and rich
chocolate orange *(see recipes,
page 93).*

HAMANTASCHEN

Cookies and fruit. Hamantaschen must have been the original Fig Newtons, except that these Purim delicacies are usually stuffed with poppy seed paste or prune fillings and shaped like the hated Haman's triangular hat.

Hamantaschen dough causes a heated debate among pastry lovers. Purists prefer the traditionally dense, cakelike dough, while others roll out a thin, crispy pastry—almost like sugar cookie dough. Some bakers use a good sweet yeast dough, while still others substitute ground nuts for half the flour. Fillings, too, are a matter of personal preference. Traditional poppy seed (called *mohn*) and prune paste (called *lekvar*) have moved over in recent years to make room for apricot, raspberry, peanut butter, date, and even chocolate chip fillings. Many appropriate canned fillings can be purchased at your local market. We've presented some very different flavors for your hamantaschen cookie basket. Nestle a batch into a pretty basket, perhaps with some fresh fruit and teabags. Line the basket with a beautiful linen napkin and twist some silk ivy around the handle for a special *shalach manot* gift presentation. Don't forget—let the children deliver the baskets, especially to senior adults whose own grandchildren live far away. The look of pleasure on their faces will warm you and your children long after Purim is past.

If you love linzertorte cookies, we suggest you make more than one batch of these pecan raspberry hamantaschen. The sweet raspberry filling is blended with the distinctive richness of pecans, and the dough is crisp and light with a delicate crunch. Our marriage of chocolate and orange uses the zest of the fruit in the dough and heavy cream in the chocolate filling to create a Purim confection that's enough to make a chocolate lover swoon—we promise.

HAMANTASCHEN TIPS

• When making multiple batches using different fillings, use the same filling flavor per cookie sheet. Different fillings require different timing, and segregating your flavor batches ensures even, just right baking.

• Be prepared to reinforce your pinched corners with beaten egg or water. Moisten the two sides before you press together, so that when the cookie expands in the oven, Haman's "hats" will still look like triangles when they're finished baking.

• Brush the cookies with a beaten-egg glaze before baking for a golden color and shiny cookie.

• Remember to tuck at least two hamantaschen into each *shalach manot* basket you prepare, as one of the two types of prepared food you should give.

• Keep your favorite hamantaschen recipe close all year long. You've probably noticed that most upscale, New York–style bakeries offer these treats all the time, not just at Purim. A plate of hamantaschen will bring Purim memories of parties, costumes, celebration, and unbridled fun, even on a dreary, drippy day in November.

PURIM MEAL

It is a custom to serve a festive meal on the afternoon of Purim, after hearing the Megillah reading for the second time in synagogue. Invite friends to enjoy an elegant yet easygoing meal that serves as a late luncheon but is hearty enough for an early supper. On the table are two holiday challahs in rounds, although some creative chefs shape their challahs like Haman's triangular hat. Note our new-fashioned place cards: we borrowed color snapshots of each guest from our photo album, ganged them together on a color copy, and slipped them into picture frames. It's a thoughtful, out-of-the-ordinary table garnish that doubles as a take-home party favor.

MENU

TRIO OF
CHOPPED SALADS:
ISRAELI,
CABBAGE SLAW,
WATERCRESS
AND AVOCADO

CHICKEN WITH WILD
MUSHROOMS AND
ARTICHOKES

ROASTED ONION AND
GARLIC KASHA
VARNISHKES

GLAZED CARROTS

CHALLAH

PAREVE
HAMANTASCHEN

A magic mélange of flavor—chicken, wild mushrooms, and artichokes. They're together in a main course that's delicious, visually appealing, and may be prepared a day or two ahead. We've teamed the chicken with kasha varnishkes that definitely isn't your mother's recipe—ours are tossed with roasted onion and garlic and laced with green herbs for extra color and flavor. Glazed carrots add a touch of sweetness and a nice punch of color to this festive meal. About the chopped salads: Guests love side dishes to sample, so we're suggesting three "can't fail" favorites. Israeli salad is a snap and tastes even better the second day. Our cabbage slaw is a version of the classic coleslaw but sweeter, since the onion macerates in sugar for thirty minutes before being tossed with the rest of the ingredients. And our avocado and watercress salad is tossed with the best olive oil you can find and flavored with fresh-squeezed lemon.

Put your table into the proper Purim spirit with unusual masks, suspended from the over-the-table light fixture with silvery metallic threads. Pick up half a dozen "magic wands" at the party shop and poke them carefully into your floral arrangement, gently pulling out the long silver and gold streamers from each wand toward each place setting. If you're brave or haven't had enough Purim merriment, place a basket of brightly colored metal graggers at each end of the table to get everyone into the party mood. For dessert, serve iced vodka and an assortment of flavored cordials in lively, tiny etched glasses with coffee and a heaping platter of our special pareve hamantaschen.

Crisp chicken breasts, crowned with an earthy mix of wild mushrooms and artichokes, are balanced beautifully with glazed carrots and nouveau kasha varnishkes tossed with roasted onions and garlic.

TRIO OF CHOPPED SALADS

Israeli Salad
SERVES 6

3 medium tomatoes, cut into ¼-inch dice
2 cucumbers, peeled and cut into ¼-inch dice
1 green pepper, cut into ¼-inch dice
2 scallions, diced fine
1 can chickpeas, rinsed and drained
2 teaspoons chopped garlic
3 tablespoons chopped parsley and mint
¼ cup vegetable oil
3 tablespoons fresh lemon juice
Salt and pepper to taste

1. Toss all vegetables in a bowl.
2. Add remaining ingredients and mix well. Refrigerate until ready to serve.

Cabbage Slaw
SERVES 6

1 medium chopped onion
1 cup sugar
1 cup vegetable oil
½ cup cider vinegar
⅓ cup mayonnaise
½ teaspoon celery seed
1 medium head of cabbage, shredded coarsely
3 carrots, shredded coarsely

1. In a bowl, combine chopped onion with the sugar. Let sit for 30 minutes.
2. Combine the oil, cider vinegar, mayonnaise, and celery seed. Mix well.
3. Combine the onion and sugar mixture with the mayonnaise mixture. Store, covered, until serving time.
4. Mix cabbage with carrots and toss with dressing right before serving.
5. Store unused dressing in refrigerator for future use.

Watercress and Avocado Salad
SERVES 6

½ cup olive oil
2½ tablespoons lemon juice
Salt and pepper to taste
5 bunches watercress, leaves only, washed and dried
2 avocados, halved, seeded, and peeled

1. Whisk olive oil and lemon juice together. Season to taste with salt and pepper.
2. Chop watercress into bite-size pieces. Toss with dressing.
3. Slice avocado into ½-inch cubes. Toss gently into salad and serve.

CHICKEN WITH WILD MUSHROOMS AND ARTICHOKES
SERVES 6

A terrific blending of flavors for our main-course chicken dish, with visual interest, too. Make it ahead, through step four, for carefree entertaining.

1½–2 pounds boneless, skinless chicken breasts (6 pieces)
Vegetable oil as needed
4 tablespoons flour
¼ teaspoon salt
¼ teaspoon cracked black pepper
2 large eggs
2 teaspoons olive oil
½ cup chopped shallots
2 teaspoons chopped garlic
6 cups sliced wild mushrooms (shiitake, portobello, cremini)
½ cup dry white wine
2 cups chicken stock

1 14-ounce can artichoke hearts, drained and quartered
Salt and pepper to taste
¼ cup chopped parsley

1. Gently pound chicken; reserve. Heat ½ inch of vegetable oil over medium-high heat in a large sauté pan.
2. Combine 3 tablespoons flour, salt, and pepper and place on a large plate. In a medium-size bowl, lightly beat eggs. Dredge each chicken breast in flour, shake off the excess, and then dip into the beaten eggs. Place in heated pan and cook for 3 minutes on each side or until golden brown.
3. Place chicken on a roasting pan and continue cooking in a 350°F oven until cooked through.
4. Remove oil from sauté pan and add olive oil. Add shallots and cook for 1–2 minutes over medium-high heat. Add garlic and mushrooms and sauté for 4–5 minutes or until golden brown. Sprinkle with remaining 1 tablespoon flour and continue to cook for 30 seconds. Deglaze pan with wine and stock; stir in artichokes. Bring to a boil, reduce to a simmer, and cook until sauce has thickened slightly. Season to taste with salt and pepper.
5. Serve sauce over chicken and sprinkle with fresh parsley.

ROASTED ONION AND GARLIC KASHA VARNISHKES
SERVES 6

4 tablespoons olive oil
12 cloves garlic, peeled
1 medium onion, cut in large dice
1 cup coarse kasha
1 egg, beaten
2 cups chicken broth
7 ounces bowtie egg noodles, cooked (4 cups cooked)
½ cup chopped parsley
Salt and pepper to taste

1. Preheat oven to 400°F.
2. In a small baking dish, combine 2 tablespoons oil, garlic, and onion. Toss to coat. Roast for 30 minutes or until golden and tender. When garlic and onions are cool, chop coarsely and reserve.
3. In a medium-size bowl, coat kasha with beaten egg. In a sauté pan with a tight-fitting lid, heat remaining oil and cook kasha for 3–4 minutes, making sure to separate grains. Add roasted garlic and onions and chicken broth. Bring to a boil, reduce to a simmer, and cook for 8–10 minutes or until kasha is tender and liquid has evaporated.
4. Fold in egg noodles and parsley and season with salt and pepper.

PACKING HAMANTASCHEN

Before packing your *shalach manot* baskets, protect your tender hamantaschen so that they arrive in one piece. Use decorative small tins, or inexpensive one-pound candy boxes from the party supply store. If you plan to package in plastic or cellophane, stack before you wrap, in twos, threes, or fours. Top with a pretty bow and make them a focal point of your gift basket.

PECAN RASPBERRY HAMANTASCHEN

MAKES APPROXIMATELY 3 DOZEN

A sweet offering for raspberry lovers, with the added richness of ground pecans and a crisp, light dough.

- 2 sticks unsalted butter
- ¾ cup granulated sugar
- 1 egg
- ½ teaspoon pure vanilla extract
- 2¼ cups all-purpose flour
- ¾ cup ground pecans
- 2 teaspoons baking powder
- ½ teaspoon salt
- ¾ cup good-quality raspberry jam
  Confectioners' sugar for dusting

1. Using an electric mixer, cream the butter and sugar. Add the egg and vanilla and mix until smooth.
2. In a medium-size bowl, combine flour, pecans, baking powder, and salt. Add slowly to the butter mixture and mix until combined. Wrap dough and refrigerate overnight.
3. Preheat oven to 350°F. Roll dough to ⅛ inch thickness and cut into 3-inch circles. Place a rounded teaspoon of jam in the center of each circle and bring the dough together on three sides to form a triangle. The filling in the center of the cookie should remain visible.
4. Arrange cookies on a cookie sheet that has been lightly sprayed with nonstick spray and bake for 20–25 minutes or until golden brown. Remove from oven and cool on racks.
5. Sprinkle with confectioners' sugar just before serving.

CHOCOLATE ORANGE HAMANTASCHEN

MAKES 2½ DOZEN

Chocolate lovers: Heavy cream added to the chocolate filling reminds us of a ganache. A must-try for everyone, including those who don't usually care for hamantaschen.

- 2 sticks unsalted butter
- ¾ cup granulated sugar
- 2 egg yolks
- ½ teaspoon pure vanilla extract
- 2¼ cups flour
- ½ teaspoon salt
- ½ teaspoon baking powder
- 2 teaspoons grated orange zest
- ⅓ cup heavy cream
- 8 ounces chopped semisweet chocolate

1. In a large bowl, cream together the butter and sugar until light and fluffy. Add the eggs and vanilla and beat until smooth.
2. Sift together the flour, salt, and baking powder. Slowly add to the butter mixture and mix until combined. Add the orange zest. Shape dough into a ball, wrap in plastic wrap, and refrigerate overnight.
3. In a small saucepan, heat cream until boiling. Remove from heat and stir in chocolate. Keep stirring until smooth. Refrigerate until stiff.
4. Preheat oven to 350°F. Roll dough to ⅛-inch thickness and cut into 3-inch circles. Place 1 teaspoon of chocolate filling in the center of each circle. Brush edges with water and bring the dough together on three sides to form a triangle. Place each on a lightly greased cookie sheet and bake for 12–15 minutes or until golden brown.

*This matzo, called Shemurah matzo, is handbaked and round—
just like the original matzo that the Jews took out of Egypt
more than 3,300 years ago.*

PASSOVER

PERHAPS NO OTHER HOLIDAY HAS AS STRONG A PULL on the Jewish soul as Passover. From the most observant to those with merely a nodding acquaintance with tradition, Jews everywhere are drawn to the seder table each year to retell the story of freedom and the birth of the Jewish nation. ✳ Passover is an eight-day festival that begins on the fifteenth of the month of Nisan. The events of Passover took place in the most dazzling of ancient lands, Egypt—ruled by the pharaoh, whose power was so absolute that it was impossible to leave Egypt without his permission. Here lived the Jews, enslaved generation after generation. Imagine the reaction of Pharaoh when Moses demands the release of the Jewish people. Only after a series of devastating and horrific plagues climaxed by the death of the firstborn in each Egyptian household does Pharaoh relent and allow the Jews to leave. Seven days later, blinded by rage and revenge, Pharaoh sends his army and traps the Jews against the Sea of Reeds. A final miracle splits the sea, allowing the Jews to cross on dry land but enclosing Pharaoh's army and drowning thousands of soldiers. Once-powerful Egypt now lies in ruins. ✳ Today, in preparation for Passover, Jewish homes are practically turned upside-down with an excitement that intensifies as the holiday nears. Cleaning is meticulous to ensure there are no traces of leavened bread, called *hametz,* anywhere. Since bread, cracker, and cereal crumbs lurk everywhere, pockets are emptied, drawers are dumped out, and sofa cushions are shaken. Finally, on the evening before Passover, ten pieces of *hametz* are scattered about. In an enchanting custom the pieces are searched for by candlelight and collected with a feather and wooden spoon. The next morning they are burned outside. ✳ Everyday dishes are put away, and special Passover dishes, pots, pans, utensils, and linens are set out. Matzo replaces bread and flour and is so ubiquitous that in the early 1900s the Jewish population of large American cities was calculated from the yearly matzo production at the rate of five pounds per person. ✳ The passionate pull of Passover tradition is so strong that it has been celebrated by soldiers during the Civil War, by doomed and starving Jews in the Warsaw ghetto, and American GIs in World War II. With each Passover, each of us walks in the footsteps of history, sharing the message of hope. Walk with joy.

THE SEDER TABLE

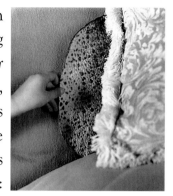

No matter how much you entertain throughout the year, this is the table setting everyone will remember. The word *seder* actually means "order"; thus at the Passover seder, unlike any other holiday meal of the year, a table is presented on which every object has a precise time and significance. Every passage in the Haggadah has its time and accompanying symbols on this table: wine, matzo, a green vegetable, bitter herbs (usually fresh horseradish root or romaine lettuce), *haroset* (a sweet paste of ground apples and nuts laced with wine), salt water, a roasted bone, a cooked egg, and the symbolic filled goblet of wine for Elijah. Three matzos must be covered and placed at the head of the table. And everyone present reads from, and asks questions from, the Haggadah, the book containing the order of the seder and chronicling the Jews' miraculous journey out of Egypt into freedom.

Because everyday dishes may not be used on Passover, many Jewish families have a special set of dishes for the seder that come out just once a year. Often they are passed down from generation to generation, but you may start a tradition by discovering dishes, stemware, flatware, linens, and unusual touches that you truly love. Tuck them away each year and see how quickly they become a cherished part of your family's history. Our frogs, for example: they represent the second plague and add a whimsical icebreaker to an otherwise formal setting. Find your four-legged amphibians at better toy stores, and place them around the table to help explain how the frogs popped up everywhere in Egypt by the millions during that plague—in beds, in ovens—driving the people to distraction.

For our seder table we chose warm tones of honeydew and gentle daffodil yellow. To further celebrate the onset of spring, our plates are majolica lookalikes with tone-on-tone raised leaves and flowers. A sheer piece of softly toned fabric over a patterned cloth adds dimension and ethereal interest.

Since the seder itself is lengthy, we suggest survival bags for your youngest guests—to keep them at the table and to keep them awake. Try a brown burlap bag containing child-pleasing props such as plastic bugs, toy frogs, a pharaoh hand puppet, and blackout sunglasses for the plague of darkness, all to illustrate the story of the Exodus.

Intervals of song keep interest high during the long hours of the seder. Many have child-friendly, repetitive lyrics that were arranged specifically to keep the non–night owls awake until the very end.

Above: A child finds the *afikomen*–the half matzo hidden at the beginning of the seder. Prizes are usually awarded to the lucky discoverer, and the matzo is eaten at the end of the seder as a final "dessert." *Opposite page:* All is in order: the resplendent seder table, waiting for guests who come to celebrate the miracle of Passover.

MATZO VASE

Your clever matzo vase will be the talk of your seder table, and you'll probably see it copied from year to year, home to home. An amusing centerpiece and perfect for the season, it takes only a few minutes to create what looks like hours of work. We've used it as a flower vase, but it works as a planter cachebox for ferns and ivies of all kinds. If you'd rather, build up the bottom and nestle a tall, fat, scented candle among silk or real blooms. For a long table with lots of guests, it's probably a good idea to make at least three vases. Either group them in the center, perhaps with a taller floral design in the center vase flanked by two candle vases, or space three along the table at intervals. These are fun hostess gifts to take to a seder and a lovely way to present any flower offering during Passover.

We've used the fragrant, lush flowers of spring for our matzo vase—in a colorful bouquet of tulips, freesia, and alstroemeria. If you're using a cut bouquet, place a short vase inside your matzo vase. If you're using potted plants, just pop in the entire pot. Make a batch of these "vases" using mini-matzos, and use them as place card holders for everyone at your table. Use clear florist's picks for the name cards and tuck among the flowers or foliage.

Pick up a box of commercial Passover matzos from your local grocery. Matzo usually arrives in the store well before the holiday, so you'll have time to experiment. You will find that most one-pound boxes of matzo contain twelve pieces, and you will need four perfect pieces

for each "vase." Buy extra to allow for breakage during shipment. You can use either the full size matzos or the minimatzos we used here. You might want to polyurethane the pieces before you glue, to make them less likely to break.

If you've never operated a

glue gun before, relax. We suggest a trigger model—they're easier to operate—and a full-size gun rather than a minigun. Buy the clear glue sticks, and when using your heated gun, rest it on an old plate or disposable pie pan. Be experimental in the greenery you use.

Boxwood is a wonderful choice. It lasts for weeks, which means you can do your arranging ahead of time. If it doesn't grow near you, your local craft or floral supply store might carry it dried. According to Jewish law, we must not waste food, so pack your vase away to use again year after year.

MATZO VASE STEP-BY-STEP

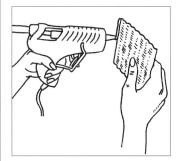

1. Using a hot glue gun, run an even strip of glue down the side of one edge of real matzo. Be careful not to drip hot wax or burn your fingers.

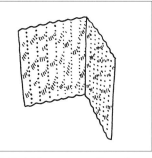

2. Quickly press another piece of matzo onto the glue at right angles, corner to corner.

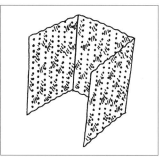

3. Add the third "wall" using the same glue-and-press method as in step two.

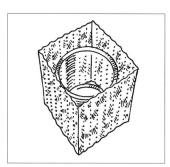

4. After adding a fourth side, hot glue a 16-oz. plastic cup (we snipped off the top ½" of the cup for fit) to the center of the vase, touching each of the four sides to the cup with hot glue.

MATZO COVER

The requisite seder accessory, with a luxe new look. According to tradition, there are at least three matzos on the Passover seder table. Called the food of faith, these flat unleavened breads were the only foodstuffs taken out of Egypt by the Jews, who trusted God to take care of them. The three matzos represent all Jews—the *Kohanim*, *Levites*, and *Israelites*. The middle matzo in the stack becomes the *afikomen*. Half is eaten at the conclusion of the seder, and the other half is hidden for the young children to find.

As the object of such an important mission, then, the matzo cover deserves a notable elegance. Ours is made of velvet, with pressed stampings for a contemporary look that's easy to achieve using decorative rubber stamps—the kind used on paper. Follow our directions for a matzo cover to give to your hosts or, better yet, to keep. After Passover, treasure your new heirloom. Gently wrap your matzo cover in plain white tissue—never plastic. Fold it after it is wrapped to keep it fresh and beautiful for years to come.

Just a few tricks will produce a professional-looking cover. It's important when choosing velvet to use the real thing—made of silk, rayon, or even acetate/rayon. Polyester or nylon lookalikes won't do, because they won't work with the stamping process and they won't last. True velvet may be expensive, but you won't need much. In fact, for a 12-inch-square cloth, one-half yard of velvet will make three. Keep one and give two away.

For the technique, we suggest working with a piece of scrap velvet until you master the heat-embossed stamping process. Use stars, family initials, or names—even Passover-themed rubber stamps from your favorite craft shop. Flower stamps are always beautiful, or you may want to stamp designs representing all the items of the seder plate—apples, parsley, a chick for the egg and bone, lettuce, and so on. Here's how it works:

1. Lightly mist the back side of your fabric with water—a plant spritzer will be fine.

2. Choose your rubber stamp and place, image side up, on an ironing board.

3. Place the velvet, right side down, against the rubber stamp, and press a medium-hot iron (no steam) onto the fabric back and hold for about 20 seconds. This should be enough time to make a 3-D permanent design in the velvet, but be prepared to adjust the iron heat and press times.

4. Check your image and continue adding the next stamp until you get the matzo cloth looking the way you want it.

5. If you like, sew on a fringed border for a formally elegant look. Use a contrasting color to add extra punch.

A nice bonus: This technique can be used on clothing, scarves, and pillows. It's unusual, looks difficult (but isn't), and opens a door of opportunity for very personalized gift giving. The sky's the limit with stamp embossing, and the only tools you need are rubber stamps, your household iron, and some creativity.

Make your own matzo cover with heat-embossed stampings on velvet. It's a beautiful project, and quick, too, even with the addition of a deep fringed border.

LIST OF MATERIALS

VELVET
½ YARD (ENOUGH FOR
3 COVERS), DEPENDING ON
THE FABRIC

HOUSEHOLD IRON

TRIGGER WATER MISTER

RUBBER STAMPS IN YOUR
CHOICE OF THEMES

FRINGE (OPTIONAL)

ELIJAH'S CUP

At every Passover seder all over the world, four cups of wine are customarily drunk in the course of the seder. A fifth cup of wine is also poured but left untouched—the cup of Elijah. Elijah was one of our greatest prophets. His spirit is considered present not just at Passover, but also at the *bris*—the circumcision ceremony—where a chair is set aside for Elijah to bless the newborn boy. Passover is universally known as the ultimate holiday of freedom. The fifth cup (Elijah's cup) has been left to be drunk when the world is ultimately freed from its wars and injustices. We will know when the time of this redemption is at hand because Elijah will have the honor of appearing to announce the arrival of the Messiah, the person sent by God to bring the world to a state of perfection and brotherhood.

Until this happens, the children will continue to open the front door wide in anticipation of his arrival and keep checking the wineglass to see if any has been drunk.

Such a prophet deserves a regal wine cup. While you can find many at local Judaica shops, our Elijah's cup is beautiful and easy to create, and we predict that it will be brought out lovingly—year after year—as a family heirloom, more precious because it came from your own heart and hands.

LIST OF MATERIALS

PLAIN WINE GOBLET

PORCELAINE PAINT BY PÉBÉO IN TUBES OR JARS

COLORED "GEMS" FROM THE CRAFT STORE

Over the past few years a number of paints have come onto the market specifically for painting permanently on glass. This ingenious process involves a drying period and a baking period in a slow oven, and the results are dazzling.

We've chosen Pébéo Porcelaine 150 Paints, a French product that produces wonderful dense tones on glass. This paint comes in jars for larger spaces and tubes for outline work.

Experiment with an old juice glass before you start with a wineglass, to get the feel of the paint, the brushes, and the surface. If you make a mistake or don't like what you've painted, wipe it off and start over. The paint isn't permanent until the baking process is completed.

The first step is to clean your goblet by washing, drying, and washing again with rubbing alcohol. Next, sketch your designs on paper and tape to the inside of the goblet, so that you're really tracing. Use your personal computer for your lettering— a fancy font in a large point size makes it easier than trying to do it freehand. Then paint your glassware and let it sit for twenty-four hours untouched. The final step is to place it in a 300°F oven for thirty-five minutes to "set" the paint permanently and make it washable. If you've used a lot of paint, you should leave your goblet in the oven for up to one hour.

Our Elijah's cup was created using round colored "gems" from the craft store and the Pébéo paint in tubes for our design and name. Let your creativity take over. Painted glass is becoming increasingly popular, and you may want to use some of the new painted florals for inspiration. You may also want to use a colored glass goblet— cobalt blue is available and very striking.

A wine cup fit for a distinguished guest like Elijah the prophet, made with special new glass paints and your own designs.

SEDER PILLOWS

A gesture of liberation, celebrated at Passover. In ancient times, reclining at a meal was the mark of a free person. Jews through the ages have reclined at the Passover seder to celebrate our ability to rest rather than toil for others without the luxury of rest. In some households the leader of the seder leans. In many other households everyone reclines. Since we are all a free people at last, we've created beautifully personal pillows for everyone at the table. When not on duty at the yearly Passover seder, they make wonderful decorator accents—in the bedroom or tucked onto a pillowed sofa. Surprise some special guests this year with these charmingly personal pillows—have them ready at their seats instead of place cards.

If you're not an experienced tailor, you may wish to buy a batch of matching pillows—one for each guest at your seder table—or have them made by a local seamstress. But if you're comfortable with pillow making—familiar with creating slip-back pillow covers and using piping—these pillows will be a snap for you. We found a professional to do our lettering by looking in the Yellow Pages under "Monogramming," but you can even use fabric paint or markers to create a special look.

To affix the finished pillows to the chairs, we pinned them on the back, then tied them to the chairs with matching ribbons.

Sending your guests home with a special seder pillow is a lovely gesture of friendship—one that tells each person how much you value his or her presence at your Passover celebration.

MAKE A SLIP-BACK SEDER PILLOW WITH PIPING

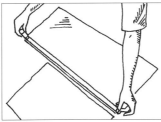

1. For the front of your pillow cover, place your purchased pillow form on the wrong side of your fabric. Cut the fabric 1 inch smaller than the finished form. For the back, add 8 inches to the width. Cut out both pieces of fabric.

2. To add piping, place purchased piping starting at the bottom of the pillowcase front raw edge to raw edge. Baste into place.

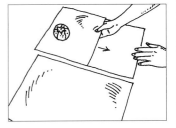

3. For the slip back, cut your fabric in half vertically, giving you two equal sections. Hem both sides of the cut by turning under ¼ inch once, then again, for a clean finish. Overlap the two pieces in the center until they match the front piece in width. Stitch into place top and bottom on your sewing machine. Then, with right sides together, place pillowcase front and back together, pin, and stitch carefully and closely right along the rise of the welt. After sewing, turn pillowcase right side out and fill with form.

You won't need place cards if your guests have their own personalized pillow. Either put away to use next Passover or let your guests take them home to throw on a bed or sofa.

105

THE SEDER MEAL

The seder plate and the chicken soup: both stir memories of other seders recently and from the long-ago past. And every morsel—from the tang of bitter herb to the comfort of matzo ball—tastes of freedom and tradition.

For the soup, a key word: pullet—an older, plumper chicken that makes incomparable soup stock, which we've teamed with a treasure of slender julienned spring vegetables. We've also updated our matzo balls with the surprise of snipped fresh herbs in honor of the spring to come.

And the seder plate: The shank bone, bitter herbs, and their companions need not be presented on the classic plate. Here, we've used square glass candle coasters fitted on a thick piece of glass from our local window glass shop.

M E N U

CHICKEN SOUP WITH
SPRING VEGETABLES AND
HERBED MATZO BALLS

ASPARAGUS SAUTÉED
WITH
LEMON AND SHALLOTS

HERB-ROASTED
RIB EYE OF BEEF
WITH PAREVE PESTO

ROASTED NEW POTATOES

VANILLA MACAROONS

SPONGE CAKE BERRY
TRIFLE

Above: Squared off for the new look in seder plates, glass candle coasters rest on a rectangle of thick glass. *Opposite page:* Fill your home with the intoxicating aroma of homemade chicken soup, dressed up for your seder with a generous julienne of spring vegetables and light matzo balls studded with fresh-snipped herbs.

Your table is resplendent, and so is your menu. Try our rib eye of beef with a luscious cloak of freshly made pesto. We've kept the main course simple, fresh, and fairly unadorned—the season's first asparagus and small, tender red potatoes.

Be certain to order your cut of beef from your kosher butcher well in advance. Because of its size and fine cut, it might not be an everyday item. Always use a meat thermometer to roast your meat to perfection. Bear in mind that meat will continue to cook even after it is removed from the oven, so check your meat thermometer often, and transfer the meat to a plate while the potatoes finish in the oven.

Because the ritual food items at the Passover seder are served before the meal, remember the need for an elegant, understated, unfussy meal. The pesto, spread on the meat, has an intensely rich, earthy flavor—a lovely prelude to the approaching spring. Garnish your platter with lots of fresh herbs. The new red potatoes have an almost sweet flavor, and the asparagus is the crowning accompaniment—wildly fresh, cooked quickly, and presented simply.

If you're lucky enough to have a guest bring a sponge cake, you may want to build a berry trifle for dessert. If not, it's easy to find prepared Passover sponge cake in your local grocery store. Straight-sided glass bowls are usually footed, and you may use clear snifters for individual trifles. Garnish with an aromatic sprig of fresh mint.

What would Passover be without macaroons? Ours couldn't be simpler—they have only four ingredients. Because these are pareve macaroons, you can serve them for dessert at your Passover seder as well as keep a batch in a tightly sealed container for nibbling all week long.

You shall eat nothing that leavens; in all your dwellings you shall eat matzos.

—SHEMOT 12:20

A little bit of pesto goes a long way, and the intense flavor marries well with many foods. Spread evenly over the roast for added flavor.

CHICKEN BROTH

SERVES 6–8

Prepare this at least one day ahead, since it needs to be refrigerated overnight.

- 1 3-pound pullet
- 3 carrots
- 2 medium onions
- 4 stalks celery
- 1 parsnip
- 1 turnip
- ½ cup washed parsley
- ½ teaspoon salt
- 5 black peppercorns

1. Place the pullet in a large stockpot. Cover with water. Add the vegetables to the pot.
2. Bring to a boil over medium heat. Skim off any foam, then reduce heat and simmer for 2 hours. Remove from heat, and remove the chicken and vegetables. Refrigerate overnight.
3. The next day, remove the fat that has settled on the top of the soup.

CHICKEN SOUP WITH SPRING VEGETABLES

SERVES 6–8

- 1 tablespoon oil
- 2 cups julienne leeks
- 2 cloves garlic, chopped
- 1 cup julienne carrots
- 1 cup julienne parsnips
- 1 cup thinly sliced celery
- 2 quarts chicken broth
- 1 teaspoon freshly chopped thyme
  Salt and pepper to taste
- 1 recipe Herbed Matzo Balls
  Fresh dill (optional)

1. Heat oil in a heavy-bottomed soup pot. Sauté leeks for 2–3 minutes, add garlic, and continue cooking for 1 minute. Add remaining vegetables and cook for 3–4 minutes. Add chicken broth and thyme. Bring to a boil and reduce to a simmer. Cook until vegetables are tender.
2. Season with salt and pepper. Place matzo balls

in soup and heat through. Serve with fresh dill if desired.

HERBED MATZO BALLS

SERVES 6–8

- 1 cup matzo meal
- 1 teaspoon kosher-for-Passover baking powder
- 1 teaspoon salt
- ½ teaspoon cracked black pepper
- 4 eggs, beaten
- ¼ cup water
- 1 tablespoon oil
- 1 tablespoon chopped fresh dill
- 2 tablespoons chopped fresh chives
- 2 tablespoons chopped fresh parsley

1. In a large bowl, mix matzo meal, baking powder, salt, and pepper. In a medium bowl, whisk together eggs, water, oil, and herbs. Add matzo meal mix and blend well. Cover and place in refrigerator for 15–20 minutes.
2. Bring a large pot of water to a boil. Shape matzo balls into golf ball size and drop into boiling water. Reduce to a simmer, cover, and cook for 30–40 minutes (no peeking!). Remove from water and place in finished chicken soup.

ASPARAGUS SAUTÉED WITH LEMON AND SHALLOTS

SERVES 6–8

- 2 pounds asparagus, cleaned and trimmed
- 1 tablespoon margarine
- 2 tablespoons chopped shallots
- 1 tablespoon lemon zest
  Salt and pepper to taste

1. Bring a large pan of water to a boil. Blanch asparagus for 2–3 minutes or until bright green and lightly tender. Remove from water and plunge into ice water. Drain and set aside.
2. Heat a large skillet with margarine. Add shallots and sauté for 3–4 minutes. Add asparagus and lemon zest, and sauté until tender. Season with salt and pepper.

PAREVE PESTO

MAKES APPROXIMATELY 1 CUP

Pesto will stay in the refrigerator for up to three weeks, and it freezes beautifully. It is wonderful to have on hand and can be used any time of the year.

- 2–3 cloves garlic, peeled
- ¼ cup walnuts
- 1 large bunch basil, cleaned and stemmed
- 1 large bunch parsley, cleaned and stemmed
- ¼ cup extra-virgin olive oil
  Salt and pepper to taste

1. In a food processor fitted with a steel blade, combine garlic and walnuts. Pulse-process until finely chopped.
2. Add basil and parsley, and puree. With the motor running, slowly drizzle in olive oil until pesto becomes emulsified. Season with salt and pepper.

HERB-ROASTED RIB EYE OF BEEF

SERVES 6–8

Use an instant-read meat thermometer to determine doneness. For medium rare meat, the thermometer should read 130°F.

- Salt and cracked black pepper
- 1 3-pound rib eye of beef
- ⅓ cup Pareve Pesto (see recipe)

1. Preheat oven to 450°F.
2. Sprinkle salt and cracked black pepper over the meat. Spread pareve pesto all over the meat, covering it entirely. Place in a roasting pan and cook for 20 minutes. Reduce heat to 350°F and continue cooking for 20–30 minutes or until desired doneness is reached.
3. Remove meat from the oven, cover loosely with foil, and let rest for 10 minutes before cutting into slices.

ROASTED NEW POTATOES

SERVES 4–6

- 2 pounds red potatoes, small baby bliss
- ¼ cup extra-virgin olive oil
- ¼ cup chopped garlic
- 2 tablespoons chopped fresh rosemary
- 1 teaspoon kosher salt
- 1 teaspoon cracked black pepper

1. Preheat oven to 375°F. In a large bowl, toss together potatoes, oil, garlic, rosemary, salt, and pepper.
2. Place on a sheet pan and bake in preheated oven for 1 hour or until potatoes are tender, tossing occasionally.

VANILLA MACAROONS

MAKES ABOUT 30

After trying these, you might never buy the canned variety again.

- **5 cups flaked sweetened coconut**
- **3 egg whites**
- **½ cup granulated sugar**
- **¼ teaspoon vanilla extract**

1. Preheat oven to 325°F.
2. Mix together all the ingredients. Make mounds about 1 inch high and 1 inch wide.
3. Place the mounds about 1 inch apart on a parchment-lined baking sheet. Bake for about 15 minutes or until the macaroons are just turning brown.

SPONGE CAKE BERRY TRIFLE

SERVES 6–8

You'll find a plethora of prepared Passover sponge cakes and boxed mixes that make this much less work than making a cake from scratch.

- **1 prepared sponge cake**
- **2 12-ounce packages of frozen mixed berries, thawed**
- **¾ cup granulated sugar**
- **4 cups nondairy whipped topping**
- **1 pint fresh berries**
  Fresh mint sprigs

1. Cut sponge cake into 12 slices; reserve. Mix thawed berries with sugar and let macerate for 1 hour.
2. To assemble, place ⅓ berry mixture in the bottom of a 2-quart bowl or trifle dish. Layer with half the cake, another ⅓ berry mixture, and whipped topping. Repeat one more time and refrigerate. (Prepare as close to the meal as possible.)
3. When ready to serve, garnish with fresh berries and mint.

Still-life with berries: Layers of cake, berries, and whipped topping look almost too pretty to eat. Be sure to use a glass trifle bowl for full visual impact.

Honor your father and your mother so that your days will be long upon the land that the Lord your God is giving to you.

—THE FIFTH COMMANDMENT

SHAVUOT

THE TEN COMMANDMENTS. Words to live by. Given in simple language and forming the blueprint of behavior for all time. Presented by God to the entire Jewish people—to each man, woman, and child. Seven weeks after the Exodus from Egypt the Jewish people stood at the foot of Mt. Sinai. There in the desert the greatest of all historical events occurred. It would take the nation forty more years to receive the entire Torah, but it began here at Sinai with the giving of the Ten Commandments. ✳ Exactly how it happened remains unimaginable, but our tradition tells us that as each commandment rang out, no birds sang, no creatures stirred, the ocean did not roar, and the Jewish people and the world changed forever. ✳ It may seem ironic that this great spiritual gift was given in a barren wasteland. But when we consider the general state of the world at that time, we see it could not have been more appropriate: human sacrifice was a widely acceptable religious practice. The killing of sick or unwanted children was commonplace. Woman were universally considered property and chattel. Acts of kindness and charity were actually considered foolish. Generally, only the rich and powerful had rights and were protected. ✳ Into this world entered the light of the Torah, with its teachings of charity and kindness to the poor, the orphan, and the stranger; its guidelines for the proper treatment of animals and the environment; and its doctrine of the infinite worth and value of every human being. With the giving of the Torah we were provided a glimpse of a perfected world and asked by God to be a partner in its achievement. Since the first Shavuot, the Jewish people have spread to the four corners of the globe. And through them, the light and teachings of the Torah have spread to all. ✳ Civilizations have come and gone. The Roman Empire has vanished. The glory of ancient Greece lies in ruins. The remnants of the pharaohs of Egypt are entombed in crumbling pyramids and glass museum cases. Sociologists and historians have wondered how the Jew, stateless and oppressed, not only survives but continues to flourish. Perhaps the answer lies in the partnership created in that first Shavuot, over 3,300 years ago.

SHAVUOT: IN FULL BLOOM

Usher in your Shavuot with a wild profusion of greenery and flowers—tubs of flowers, bowers of greenery, garlands of vine. You can't overdo it. The tradition of decorating with fresh flora comes from the holiday's secondary significance as an agricultural festival in Israel, since it falls at harvest time. Shavuot is also known as *Hag Hakatzir*, the "Festival of the Harvest," for the last grain harvest of the season, and as *Yom KaBikkurim*, the "Day of the First Fruits," for the fruit harvest.

An interesting note: The word *shavuot* means "weeks" in Hebrew, and the holiday is celebrated seven full weeks after the second day of Passover.

The timing is perfect in our part of the world. The peonies are bursting with huge, bowl-size blooms, there are wonderful greens to be gleaned in our own backyards, and the nurseries are loaded with a breathless bounty of vivid annuals and perennials in flats, pots, and containers. Trim your front hall with a lavish hand. Turn your entryway into a gorgeous greenhouse of varied texture, size, and color, and make sure some of them have a wonderful, subtle scent. Experiment with heights, too, just as you would in a flower garden—with smaller pots flanked by the bigger containers and fill-ins to tuck into any bare spots. The great news is that after Shavuot, it's practically summer, so you can pop your plants right into the ground or haul out the big potted flowers to your entryway or back to the deck or patio for a season of outdoor bloom.

Our door trim is made of magnolia leaves, left over from a spring pruning after the tree bloomed. The leaves are glossy and handsome—so are peony and andromeda leaves. The garland isn't really strung together at all. We inserted each clump of stems into plastic florist vials filled with water, then secured each vial to the door molding with green floral or plain masking tape. The florist will sell you the water vials for a nominal fee, and they'll keep your flowers or greenery fresh for days, as long as the water lasts. Another idea: Use dainty dianthus cupped with a circle of perfect violet leaves to create bouquets for a beautiful floral frame.

Create your own palette, and select your perfect space. Celebrate the spirit of the Shavuot festival in tandem with nature.

The greening of Shavuot. Fresh bursts of nature create a lush, lovely welcome for friends and family. Plantings can move right outside after the holiday for a season full of summer color.

LUMINARIES

A path strewn with stars. Light up your entrance and guide your guests to a late night Shavuot study session with these magical homemade luminaries that may be used again and again. On the fiftieth day after the Exodus from Egypt the Ten Commandments were given. Exhausted from having spent three days preparing to receive the Torah, the Jewish people were sound asleep as the appointed time neared, and God had to rouse them with great claps of thunder and bolts of lighting. Since our ancestors were almost late for the most important moment in the history of the world, we make amends for them with all-night study sessions.

Today, these study sessions take place in every community—in homes, synagogues, and schools. There are even on-line sources for Shavuot study. Host a study session in your home, with plenty of dairy treats and a pot of strong coffee. (Check our recipe for Turkish coffee—it's so robust that you might end up studying for two nights!) And set your luminaries along the steps and pathway to your home. If you live in an apartment, scatter them strategically around the living room, dining room, and kitchen—a beautiful way to light the way to Torah learning, wherever you live.

Our luminaries are easy to make. An added plus— they're safer and sturdier than the original paper bag variety. Because they're made of half-gallon milk or juice cartons, the most important tool to have is an X-Acto knife with some spare blades.

Rinse out the cartons and cut off the tops, keeping the edges as straight as possible.

Next, choose a spray-paint color for your luminaries. Place the empty cartons in a big cardboard box to keep your spray painting contained. The cartons will need several coats of paint to cover the lettering, but the spray paint dries fairly quickly. Just keep rotating the cartons for even coverage.

Draw the shapes you'd like to cut on tissue paper, or freehand them directly onto the carton. Try to stay with shapes that have straight lines, because curves are rather tricky to cut with an X-Acto knife on thick cartons. Ours is a six-pointed Star of David—all straight lines. Don't worry about perfection, either—slightly abstract shapes work best and look great. When the luminaries are finished, add two or three inches of sand to the bottom to protect them from strong winds. Nestle a fat candle into the sand—the kind that burns for hours— and you're finished. If you're using votives, put them into a glass before inserting into the sand, for extra wind protection.

Save your luminaries for all kinds of parties. They work well for cookouts and other outdoor festivities and may be used all year long to light up your walkway and steps. Now that you know how to make them, you'll want to try different shapes and top treatments. For other Jewish holidays, try the silhouette of Jerusalem. Scatter and cut square- and arch-shaped openings on each side to resemble the windows of the Holy City. Along the top, cut a notched castle look to simulate the rooflines. Spray some blue, some gold, and place along a mantel, sideboard, or your front steps for a glowing welcome.

Light up the night for Torah study with our luminaries to lead the way. All you need are some half-gallon cartons, an X-Acto knife, a bag of sand, and some tea light candles.

And God said, Let there be luminaries in the expanse of the heavens to give light upon the earth.

—BERESHIT 1:14

DAIRY MEAL

A delicious custom of Shavuot is the serving of dairy foods. Blintzes, sour cream, cheesecakes, herring in cream sauce, macaroni and cheese, and vegetable lasagna are typical offerings. And while some communities serve dairy foods only on the first day of Shavuot, others make it a complete dairy holiday.

One explanation for this custom is the commemoration of an Israel flowing with milk and honey. Another reason is that when the Jews first received the Ten Commandments on Shavuot, they were not yet well versed in the intricate laws of *shechitah* (kosher slaughtering), so rather than eat meat, they ate only dairy foods.

We've presented a deliciously different twist to the classic blintz-and-cheesecake repast, with savory herbed blintzes, a wondrous onion soup, and a cheesecake tart. Although Shavuot is a "cooking holiday," these dishes can be made days in advance to suit your time budget.

This meal is designed to be a relaxing lunch as you enjoy your friends and family, with a table laden with flowers and wonderful food that travels around the table twice—at least. Everything can be prepared ahead of time, with optimum results: the flavors of the five-onion soup mellow

A mélange of flavors for Shavuot, from a hearty onion soup to blintzes bound with herbs, ending lightly with a pretty cheesecake tart.

and intensify, and the sweet and crunchy components of the spinach and orange salad marry with time. Make your blintz wraps in advance. Make a big batch and stack them, one by one, with waxed paper sandwiched between each. Tuck the piles of blintzes into plastic food storage bags and refrigerate for up to three days, or freeze for a week or two ahead of time. Even the cheesecake tarts can be made a few days ahead and refrigerated.

> **MENU**
>
> FIVE-ONION SOUP
>
> SAVORY HERBED BLINTZES WITH ROASTED RED PEPPER SAUCE
>
> SPINACH AND ORANGE SALAD
>
> CHEESECAKE TARTS
>
> COFFEE AND TEA

FIVE-ONION SOUP

SERVES 6

Top this soup with a slice of French bread that has been brushed with olive oil and toasted. Sprinkle with 2 tablespoons of shredded Swiss cheese and broil until hot and bubbly.

2 tablespoons butter
3 cups sliced Spanish onions
3 cups sliced purple onions
2 cups sliced leeks
1 cup sliced shallots
⅓ cup (10 cloves) sliced garlic
2 tablespoons flour
6 cups vegetable broth
1 bay leaf
½ cup Marsala wine
⅓ cup chopped fresh parsley
Salt and pepper to taste

1. Heat butter in a heavy-bottomed soup pot. Add Spanish onion, purple onion, leeks, shallots, and garlic. Sauté for 12–15 minutes over medium heat or until onions become golden brown.
2. Sprinkle onions with flour and mix well to incorporate. Cook for 1–2 minutes. Add vegetable broth and bay leaf. Bring to a boil and reduce to a simmer. Cook for 20–25 minutes. Remove bay leaf and stir in Marsala and parsley. Season with salt and pepper.

SAVORY HERBED BLINTZES

MAKES 16 BLINTZES

WRAPS
3 eggs
1¼ cups milk
1 cup flour
½ teaspoon salt
2 tablespoons melted butter
No-stick cooking spray

FILLING
1 tablespoon plus 1–2 tablespoons as needed for sautéing
1½ cups diced red onions
2 cloves garlic, chopped
1 pound farmer's cheese
⅔ cup chopped parsley
¼ cup chopped basil
¼ cup freshly grated Parmesan cheese
1 egg, beaten
½ teaspoon cracked black pepper
1 egg white, beaten

To prepare wraps:

1. In a medium-size bowl, whisk together eggs, milk, flour, and salt, until smooth. Stir in butter and blend well. Cover and place in refrigerator for 30 minutes.
2. Heat an 8-inch nonstick skillet with cooking spray. Place 2–3 tablespoons of batter in pan and quickly coat entire bottom of pan. Cook for 1 minute, flip, and continue cooking for 30 seconds. Place on waxed paper and repeat with remaining batter.

To prepare filling:

3. Melt 1 tablespoon butter in a medium-size sauté pan. Add onions and cook for 2–3 minutes or until golden brown and soft. Add garlic and continue cooking for 30 seconds. Remove from pan and place in large mixing bowl. Fold in farmer's cheese, parsley, basil, Parmesan cheese, egg, and pepper. Mix well.

To assemble blintzes:

4. On a clean work surface, place 2 rounded tablespoons of filling in the center of each blintz. Fold the two lateral sides into the center. Brush upper end with egg white and roll up from the bottom. Repeat with remaining ingredients.
5. Heat 1–2 tablespoons of butter in a medium-size sauté pan and cook 3–4 blintzes for 2–3 minutes on each side or until golden and crispy. Repeat with remaining blintzes. Serve with Roasted Red Pepper Sauce. Recipe follows.

ROASTED RED PEPPER SAUCE

MAKES 3 CUPS

This sauce freezes beautifully. It is wonderful served with grilled fish or tossed in pasta.

1 tablespoon olive oil
1 cup sliced onions
2 cloves garlic, minced
2 12-ounce jars roasted red peppers, drained and roughly chopped (or 4 medium peppers, roasted, skinned, and chopped)
½ cup vegetable broth
Salt and pepper to taste

1. In a medium-size saucepan, heat olive oil. Add onions and sauté for 3–5 minutes. Add garlic and cook for an additional minute.
2. Add roasted peppers and vegetable broth. Bring to a boil, reduce to a simmer, and cook for 10–12 minutes.
3. Puree sauce in either a blender or a food processor until smooth. Season with salt and pepper.

SPINACH AND ORANGE SALAD

SERVES 8

2 tablespoons plus 2 teaspoons sugar
1 cup pecans
½ head iceberg lettuce, cleaned and torn into bite-size pieces
½ head romaine lettuce, cleaned and torn into bite-size pieces
1 cup chopped celery
4 scallions, chopped
2 11-ounce cans mandarin oranges, drained

DRESSING
1 teaspoon salt
1 teaspoon pepper
4 tablespoons sugar
4 tablespoons vinegar
8 shakes Tabasco sauce
2 tablespoons chopped parsley
½ cup olive oil

1. Over low heat, caramelize the sugar and pecans. Set on waxed paper to harden and set aside.
2. Mix together the dressing ingredients except for the olive oil. Slowly whisk in the olive oil until well mixed. Refrigerate until serving.
3. Mix ahead all salad ingredients and refrigerate until time to serve.
4. Just before serving, toss salad with dressing and nuts and mix well.

peel, sugar, and flour and pulse-process until combined. Place ⅓ cup of batter into each tart pan and bake in preheated oven for 25–30 minutes or until set.

6. Cool tarts overnight in refrigerator. Decorate with fresh berries and brush with melted apricot jam, if desired.

TURKISH COFFEE

SERVES 4

8 teaspoons finely ground dark roast coffee

4 teaspoons sugar

½ cup cold water

1. Place the coffee and sugar in a small saucepan. Add water and heat over medium-high heat.

2. After the coffee comes to a gentle boil, a dark crust will form on the top of the foam.

3. Simmer a few more minutes, then pour into small cups. Serve immediately.

Using *kichel* instead of traditional graham crackers gives this crust a different taste and texture.

CHEESECAKE TARTS

MAKES 8 TARTS

8 sugarcoated *kichel*

½ cup unsalted butter, melted

1 pound cream cheese, softened

1 cup sour cream

3 eggs

½ teaspoon vanilla extract

1 teaspoon freshly grated lemon peel

¾ cup superfine sugar

2 tablespoons flour

Fresh berries (optional)

Apricot jam (optional)

1. Preheat oven to 300°F.

2. Grease eight 4-inch tart pans.

3. Break up *kichel* into bite-size pieces and place in the bowl of a food processor that has been fitted with a steel blade. Pulse-process *kichel* until mixture resembles fine crumbs. Place in a medium-size bowl and mix well with melted butter.

4. Place ⅓ cup crumbs in each tart pan and press along sides and bottom of pan. Bake in a preheated oven for 12–15 minutes or until crumbs begin to set. Remove from oven.

5. Place cream cheese in the bowl of a food processor and process until smooth. Add sour cream, eggs, and vanilla. Scrape down sides of bowl in order to achieve a smooth mixture. Add lemon

*With the lighting of the Shabbat candles on Friday night,
our homes become filled with tranquillity and joy—
for now the Shabbat has begun.*

SHABBAT

A true story about the Shabbat goes like this: A young boy, eight-year-old Schneur Zalman,* sat outside the door of his father's study some 250 years ago, listening to the great rabbis of his town as they pondered a difficult hypothetical question: If a person is shipwrecked, unconscious, and alone on a desert island, how will this person know when the seventh day of the week, the Shabbat, has come? Opinions were many, but not one of these wise men had a conclusive answer. Unable to contain himself any longer, little Schneur Zalman burst into the room, saying, "Why is this a problem? You only need to look at the sky, because everyone can see the light is different on Shabbat." ☀ Today, few of us have the small boy's spiritual insight. But Shabbat truly is different from the other days of the week. The table shines with our best silver and crystal. Extra places are set for guests. Shabbat candles glow and parents murmer blessings over their children. The rituals of Shabbat, deposited in the collective memories of Jews throughout the ages, are alive and well after thousands of years. The sweet first taste of wine and the first bite of fresh challah after the prayers. Shabbat songs, called *zimiros*, sung around the table as dessert is finished. And the peaceful knowledge that pressing matters left over from the week before will simply have to wait. Because Shabbat is truly an island in time. A time to rest, revitalize, and enjoy family and friends. A time to unplug the phone, leave mail unopened, and keep the car in the garage. A time to put serious decisions and discussions on hold. It seems difficult, perhaps, in our complicated lives to imagine such a concept. But perhaps this is why Jewish people are enthusiastically embracing Shabbat in such large numbers today—it makes perfect sense. ☀ You might not have the ability to see that the light is different on Shabbat, but on these pages we will show you some beautiful ways to enhance your Shabbat experience at home, in a most personal way—from Friday evening candlelighting to the havdalah service. *Shabbat Shalom.*

* Schneur Zalman became the first rebbe of the Lubavitch-Chabad-Hasidim.

CHALLAH

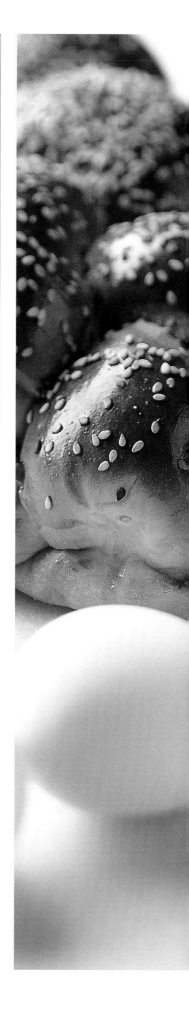

If bread is life, then challah is the sweet hereafter. Walk into a kosher bakery on Friday morning and the aroma of fresh challah can practically lift you off your feet. The physical beauty of plump, braided loaves, shiny with egg glaze and dusted with seeds, is capable of stirring thoughts of home, family, and Friday nights—past and present.

You can create the same pleasure zone at home by baking your own challah. Your touch, your effort, make it a spiritual experience, as you physically prepare for Shabbat. Your own way with challah makes yours unique, shaping the memories for the next generation and the next.

Always use two challahs on your Shabbat table. These two loaves symbolize the double portion of manna given to the Jews on the sixth day of each week during their years of wandering in the desert. This extra portion was provided by God so that the Jews could observe the laws of the Sabbath completely, without having to prepare food.

Without exaggeration, there is no bread quite like challah. Its smooth texture, and almost cakelike flavor make it a favorite treat to usher in the Sabbath and has earned it quite a healthy following in the non-Jewish world as well.

Traditional Shabbat challahs are braided into loaves or coiled deftly into small shapes for rolls or individual twists. The dough is shaped into large rounds for holidays, sometimes with the addition of raisins. There are many recipes, too. Yellow egg challahs compete with lighter water, or eggless, challahs. Whole wheat is gaining favor among some challah fans. Some bakers use honey instead of sugar; others add extra egg yolks for a richer golden color, and the addition of poppy or sesame seeds is a matter of personal preference.

If two loaves prove to be too much each week, try these pleasurable solutions: Make the best French toast in the universe with fat slices of leftover challah dipped in a mixture of eggs, milk, vanilla, and cinnamon and dusted with powdered sugar. Use leftovers for bread pudding, mankind's ultimate comfort food. Or toast the slices in a slow oven for several hours, season, and drop into the food processor for a bountiful supply of bread crumbs. (Seeded challahs are fine—they add a nice, nutty crunch.)

Another solution—and this one's good for the soul: Practice the mitzvah of *hachnasat orchim*—inviting guests for Shabbat dinner, especially those who aren't yet accustomed to the tradition or those whose schedules does not allow them to prop-

erly prepare a meal for Shabbat. You certainly won't have to worry about leftover challah.

Challah makes a special gift for friends, too—nestled in a napkin-lined basket with jams, some cheese, tangy Israeli olives, and some wine or grape juice. It's a warm, comforting way to welcome new neighbors to your community or synagogue, a guaranteed mood lifter for ill or recovering friends, or a nice way to thank a friend for just being there.

Remember, don't be intimidated by the baking process. Our recipe and step-by-step instructions will help you sail through your challah baking like a pro, even if you've never baked bread before. We hope it will be the beginning of a delicious new tradition in your home.

CHALLAH 101

Each time a present-day Jewish household bakes challah in preparation for Shabbat, the link to our ancestors is strengthened. The tie that binds the centuries of generations is as supple and alive as the dough itself.

From ancient times, when the Jewish people first lived in the land of Israel, they were commanded to give the *Kohanim*, or priestly tribe, many gifts. One of these was a portion of their dough each time they baked bread. This was called *challah*, as it is today. In fact, it is still the custom, when baking batches of bread using more than twelve cups of flour, to break off a small (one-ounce) portion of dough to symbolize this ancient gift. Because we can no longer give this to the *Kohanim*, and we shouldn't use it ourselves, it is customary to burn it separately on a piece of foil under the broiler or over a gas burner. This is one mitzvah unique to women. The accompanying prayer is sacred and beautiful, and if we close our eyes and listen hard, we can hear our own voices join those of our mothers and sisters from so long ago.

CHALLAH TIPS

• Don't kill your yeast with too hot water, a common error for first-timers. The water should be tepid. If it feels the same temperature as your skin, it's fine.
• Try substituting a cup of honey for the sugar.
• Add a few drops of yellow food coloring to the liquid ingredients for a richer, "eggier" look without the extra cholesterol.
• Don't skimp on the salt called for in the recipe. Along with the yeast, sugar, and water, it's an important part of a chemical process that allows the dough to rise properly.
• Don't rush the rising process. The first rising takes longer than the second; cover your dough with a thick cotton napkin or towel, and place in a warm location. A sunny window, warm hearth, or stovetop is a good choice. Or heat your oven and turn off, then place your bowl in the still-warm oven with the door open.
• Immediately after pulling challahs from the oven, transfer to cooling racks to prevent soggy bottoms.
• For holiday round challahs, try baking them in round cake pans for a picture-perfect look.
• The recipe given makes extra challahs. To freeze, pop hot challahs into paper bags. Put the paper bags into plastic freezer bags and twist tie. After thawing, remove from bags and heat in the oven for 10 minutes for a just baked flavor and texture.

BASIC CHALLAH
MAKES APPROXIMATELY
4 LOAVES

4 packages dry yeast
3½ cups warm water
½ cup sugar
1¼ teaspoons salt
13–14 cups flour
5 eggs, beaten
1 cup vegetable oil
1 egg, beaten with 1 teaspoon of honey, for glaze
Poppy or sesame seeds (optional)

1. In a large bowl, sprinkle yeast over warm water and let sit until it dissolves.
2. Add sugar, salt, and half the flour. Mix well.
3. Stir in the eggs and oil; add the remaining flour slowly.
4. Turn out dough onto a floured board and knead for 10 minutes. If dough is too moist, add a little more flour.
5. When ready to rise, put dough in a large bowl, smear top with oil, cover, and let rise for 1 hour.
6. Separate small "challah portion" of dough.
7. Braid remaining dough into a loaf and let rise for 1 hour. Brush with egg glaze; sprinkle with seeds if desired.
8. Bake in a preheated oven at 350°F for 1 hour or until golden brown.

CHALLAH STEP-BY-STEP

1. Sprinkle yeast over warm water and let sit until it dissolves.

2. Add the sugar, salt, and half the flour.

3. Add the eggs and oil. Then add the remaining flour slowly.

4. Put in a large bowl. Smear top with oil, cover, and let rise for 1 hour. Separate the small "challah portion." Shape and braid remaining dough; let rise another hour. Brush with beaten egg glaze, sprinkle with seeds, and bake at 350°F for 1 hour.

BRAIDING STEP-BY-STEP

Add an extra twist to your challahs with an expert 4-part braid.

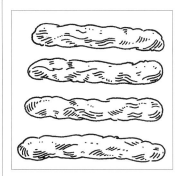

1. If you can make a 3-part braid, you can manage a fourth. Divide dough into 4 equal parts and roll each into 20" ropes or as long as you can make them.

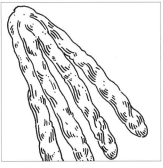

2. Place the ropes side by side, and press the tops together. You may want to "stick" them together by brushing on some water or beaten egg glaze.

3. Grasp the left rope and weave it under the rope beside it, over the one next to that, and under the following rope—a technique reminiscent of the woven pot holders we made in nursery school.

4. Start again with the new rope, weaving over, under, and over. Do it twice again until your weaving is finished. Take the ends, press to connect, and tuck them under the loaf.

ROUND CHALLAH STEP-BY-STEP

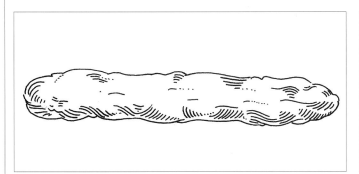

1. Roll out a long rope of dough, about 20" long and 3" wide. One end should be thicker than the other.

2. Use the thick end as the center, and coil the remaining dough around the center. Tuck the outside end underneath the challah.

Challah Cover

Golden braids of challah, nestled in pairs on the Shabbat table. These lovely loaves are hidden by a beautifully ornamental cloth that gets lifted every time someone passes through the dining room. There's history, of course, surrounding the two challahs and the challah cloth.

Each Friday during the Jews' journeying in the desert, a double portion of food, called *manna*, fell from the heavens so that they would not have to gather food on the Shabbat. This mysterious food—which many rabbinic authorities believe to have been small, rounded, and waferlike—was covered with a layer of dew to keep it fresh. The two loaves of challah represent the double portion of manna, and the challah cloth symbolizes the dew that protected the manna.

Our challah cloth, in an elegant, natural raw silk, is strewn with tiny pearls to remind us of the dew on the manna. Ours is a pleasant, uncluttered change from some of the more traditional challah cloths that are available commercially.

And may God give to you of the dew of the heavens and of the fatness of the earth and plenty of grain and wine.

—BERESHIT 27:28

We were lucky to find an oversize raw silk napkin, so we didn't even have to hem a piece of fabric. Beautiful single napkins can be found on clearance tables at kitchen or department stores for very little money, and they're just the size you need for a great challah cover. For the pearly look, we broke apart an old necklace and sewed on the beads. If you don't care to sew, use a sturdy jewelry glue. We marked off every three inches with some tailor's chalk before we affixed the pearls. The result was uniform—and fabulous.

For the corners, an assemblage of pearls and pretend gold—these from two pairs of pierced pearl-drop earrings attached to each corner for weights—and lots of compliments. Silky tassels work nicely, too, and can be sewn on in just a moment or two. If you're handy with the sewing machine, purchase several raw silk remnants and sew together one-inch-by-twelve- or (sixteen-) inch strips for a contemporary, coordinated look. Create your own designs with contrasting silk, and use the appliqué stitch on your sewing machine to outline the shapes onto the cover. It's up to you—just usher in the Shabbat with fragrant challahs and a cover of your own choosing.

Cover your challah with a designed-by-you cover of raw silk strewn with tiny sewn-on pearls.

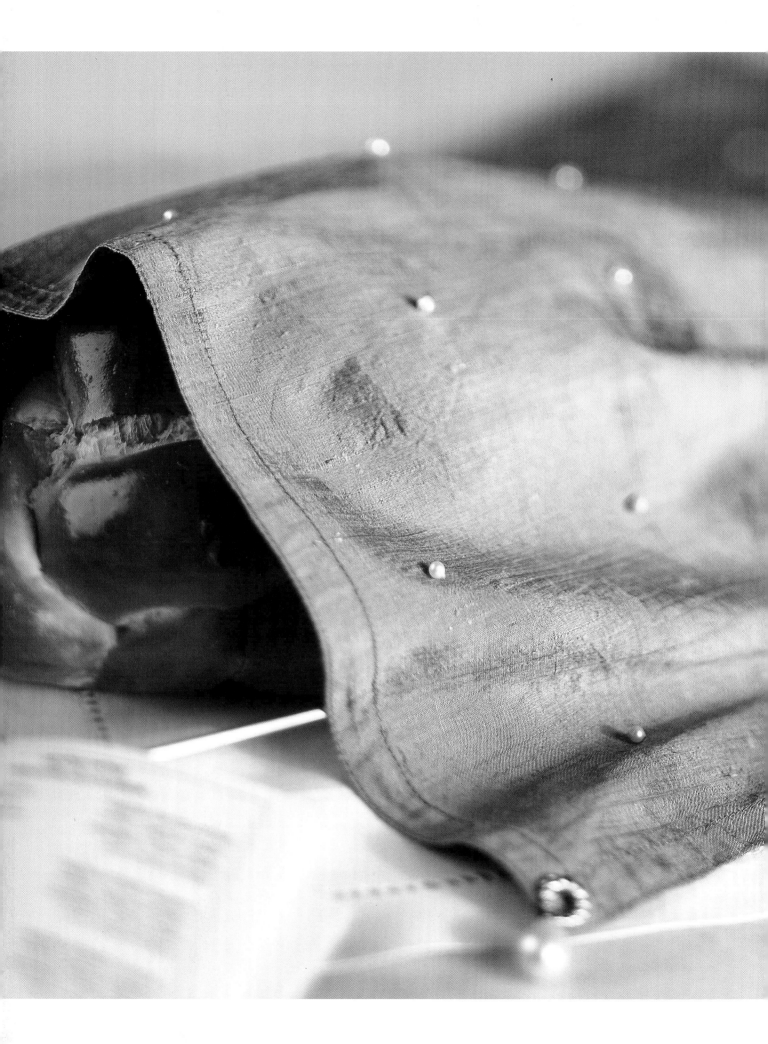

SHABBAT CANDLESTICKS

The lighting of Shabbat candles, which signifies the beginning of the Sabbath, has enjoyed a renaissance in recent years. The reason? Perhaps this Friday night tradition symbolizes the soothing close of a harried week for many families. It could be just to enjoy the excitement with which their young children look forward to the ceremony each week. Or it might be that the candle-glow and soft prayers whispered create an undeniable tie that binds us to our past as we hurtle into the future.

From a spiritual point of view, candles are said to symbolize domestic harmony, dedication to God, Torah and mitzvot, and the triumph of good. It is said that when the candles are lit, the home is bathed in peace and holiness, warmth and unity.

Traditionally, married women light at least two candles. Many have adopted the custom of lighting an additional candle for each of their children. Single women light one candle, and so do young girls from the age of three or as soon as they learn the blessing recited at candlelighting. A few coins are usually dropped into the *tzedakah* box before lighting. Lighting is done eighteen minutes before sunset or up to the sunset each Friday afternoon. The time is published in your town's local Jewish newspaper, or you may call your favorite synagogue for a candlelighting chart to keep at home. As you light your candles, appreciate that you are joining the wave of Jewish women who are kindling their candles as the sun falls, working its way around the world.

It is customary to use special candlesticks for the mitzvah of Shabbat candlelighting. If you like the idea of having truly unique candlesticks, you might want to try this pretty pair, complete with a matching tray. Use unfinished wooden candlesticks from the craft store, as we did, or recycle a ho-hum pair in plain glass or metal that you already own.

We used 6-millimeter flat-

A creamy glow emanates from these pearled candlesticks created by you for your special Shabbat tradition.

back "pearls," ordered from a New York costume jewelry supplier (see our source guide in the back of this book), but any favorite finish will be lovely—jewel tones, faux onyx or hematite, even some frosted jewel tones. The flat backs are easier to work with than full round shapes, and they ensure a smooth, uniform finish.

Use Aleene's Jewel-It glue from the craft store to affix your pearls. It dries clear and tacks instantly, preventing the pearls from sliding around while you're arranging

them. Another plus—Jewel-It dries to a shiny, clear finish, giving your piece a painlessly professional look.

To complete the design, we glued pearls around a simple silverplated tray. Trimming a silverplated matchbox would be a fitting finishing touch. One tip: We suggest the use of glass candle rings to avoid dripping wax on your pearled candlesticks. They are available everywhere and actually enhance the look of your candlesticks.

Remember that once Shabbat candles are lit, they

must not be moved, so pick a safe spot where they can burn undisturbed for several hours. A dining room sideboard is a popular spot in many homes.

While originally Shabbat candles were designed for use—to bring light into the home—today they bring not only light, but peace and harmony, too.

If you haven't lit Shabbat candles lately, please join your worldwide Jewish family in this special tradition. Add your light to ours as the blessings of your ancestors warm your Shabbat.

HAVDALAH SPICE BOX

Just as the Shabbat queen is ushered in with great ceremony, she is given a special farewell as well, with the recitation of havdalah services. Havdalah may take place anytime after night fall in the synagogue or at home on Saturday evening. The departure of Shabbat, with its peace, rest, and family togetherness, is somewhat wistful and melancholy. The havdalah ceremony serves as a separation between Shabbat and the weekdays. Wishes for a *shavuah tov*—good week—are liberally dispensed with a sip of wine and a heady whiff of fragrant spices. This beautiful ceremony, precious in many Jewish homes, has its own paraphernalia: the multiwicked havdalah candle, a small tray bearing a wine cup, and a spice or fragrance box.

There are, of course, reasons for each of these. Wine signifies joy and gladness, and honors holidays and special occasions. The sweet fragrances are a delight for the soul, and a compensation for the departure of Shabbat. The lighting of the havdalah candle is to remind us of the first act of creation when God said, "Let there be light." It also symbolizes taking the light of Shabbat with us into the week ahead, and thus should be a strong torchlike flame, which requires multiwicked candles that are usually braided. Children love to take part in the ceremony by carefully holding the havdalah candle.

The spice containers are usually made of silver, olive wood, or brass and often filled with cloves, cinnamon, or ginger. Create your own spice mix or fill your box with a favorite potpourri blend. Sephardic Jews use fragrant rosewater in small vessels that resemble samovars. In keeping with this ancient tradition, we chose rose petals, tucked into an elegant box that's easy to make.

Our sensational spice box started as an unfinished wooden box from the craft store. If you prefer another shape, a metal canister works, too. We used the old technique of decoupage with an updated mix of stripes and a floral to give the spice box a luxe look. Essentially, decoupage is simply the process of gluing paper onto a surface and giving it a matte or shiny finish. The paper has a tight cling, which becomes the finish on the piece. Choose your patterns from

tissue papers, wonderful luncheon napkins, or artful gift wrappings, available in every conceivable look these days. We used a floral for the top of the box and strips of white and tan for the bottom stripes. Use either a glue made for decoupage projects or white glue that's been thinned down a bit with water. Brush the glue onto the box and lay the box onto the paper you've rough-cut to generously cover the box— you'll fine-tune the trimming later. Wrap the piece with the

paper, and don't worry about creasing. It only adds dimension and texture to the finished piece. After the glue dries stiff, use an X-Acto knife, single-edge razor blade, or tiny scissors to cut away the excess paper. Rough or extra edges may be reglued and smoothed down with your finger. There's really no wrong way to use this decoupage method.

When everything is thoroughly dry, place the box in a large cardboard box and give it a clear coat of spray var-

nish. Add a wonderful trim from your favorite fabric store with a hot glue gun. Since you'll love the way this havdalah box turns out, we should tell you that the decoupage method works well on flowerpots, wastebaskets, even furniture, for an eclectic but elegant decorating lift.

Above: **A braided havdalah candle creates a torch with its multiple wicks. *Opposite page:* A sweet way to end your Shabbat—with fragrant rose petals in an elegant decoupaged box.**

SHABBAT SHIRAH

This little-known Shabbat connects us to nature, with a special nod to the birds. It always takes place in the winter, when birds could use a nourishing meal. The story of Shabbat Shirah takes us back to the Exodus, when the Jews were crossing the desert out of Egypt. Every day the people went out from the camp to gather the manna that God sent down from the heavens for food. At God's command, Moses instructed the people to take a double portion on Friday, as none would be sent on Shabbat. This was to avoid having to go out from the camp and gather on Shabbat. Like all great leaders, Moses had his enemies. Two men, Dasam and Avirom, arose early on Shabbat and secretly put out the remaining portions of their Friday manna. Then, to discredit Moses, they returned later with a number of people to prove to them that God had sent more manna on the Shabbat. However, their manna was gone, as God had sent birds to eat what they had put out. From that time on, the birds were acknowledged as messengers from God on Shabbat Shirah. Another reason we feed the birds is that they sang along with the Jews as they left Egypt—the word *shirah* means "to sing."

The birds in your yard will appreciate your gift—a homemade birdseed ball that is sure to attract a rainbow of flying visitors. Make a batch and hang half a dozen seed balls on the bare branches of a favorite tree—near a window, of course.

BIRDSEED BALLS

1 cup vegetable shortening
1 cup peanut butter
3 cups cornmeal
¼ cup chopped nuts
¼ cup raisins
¼ cup birdseed

1. Mix everything together in a large bowl, using your hands.
2. Form into balls and chill for an hour for easier handling.
3. When the balls are chilled, place into the center of squares of net and tie with a ribbon.
4. Hang outdoors for your feathered friends.

In cold northern climates especially, birds need the extra nutritional boost from a backyard bird feeder. They're not fussy eaters, either—your stale cake, bread, and doughnuts provide the essential fat they need to stay warm during harsh weather. Leftover pasta, rice, and pet food provide nutrients, too. Birds come to feed in shifts—there really is a pecking order in the bird kingdom—and each batch of birds provides colorful, ever-changing scenery on a dreary winter's day.

A few things to remember: Once you start feeding the birds in winter, continue until spring. They come to depend on you for food, and they make your bird feeder a part of their daily routine. If you stop feeding them suddenly, they could starve.

To discourage pesky squirrels who regularly rob your feeders, sprinkle cayenne pepper on your birdseed balls or other treats. The squirrels loathe the peppery taste, but the birds don't seem to mind it at all.

Treat your winged friends to homemade birdseed balls on Shabbat Shirah.

HOLIDAY HIGHLIGHTS

The complete presentation of the myriad details for observing the Jewish holidays is beyond the scope of this work. Although highlights are presented here, the reader should consult competent rabbinic authorities for prayers and more information. Of the holidays presented, Rosh Hashanah, Yom Kippur, Sukkot, Simchat Torah, Passover, Shavuot, and Shabbat are of biblical origin, having been decreed in the written Torah. They all have common elements of candlelightings, kiddush, and festive meals. The remaining holidays, Chanukah, Tu B'Shvat, and Purim, are of rabbinic origin, having been decreed by the Sages to commemorate events that occurred after the Torah was written. These holidays have unique and wonderful customs and rituals.

ROSH HASHANAH

- Candlelighting both nights
- Kiddush and festive meals, both nights and days
- Hear the blowing of the shofar in synagogue
- *Tashlich* first afternoon except on Sabbath
- Dip apple or challah in honey
- Pomegranates are served to remind us to do many mitzvahs, as the fruit has many seeds

YOM KIPPUR

- Two festive meals (without kiddush)
- Extra *tzedakah*
- *Yahrzeit* candles
- Candlelighting before sunset
- Go to synagogue and pray
- Wear white to synagogue to symbolize purity
- Fast the entire day from the previous sundown

SUKKOT

- Candlelighting first two nights. Kiddush and festive meals first two nights and days
- Eat in sukkah as much as possible
- Perform the mitzvah of *lulav* and *etrog*

SIMCHAT TORAH

- Candlelighting both nights
- Kiddush and festive meal both nights, the first eaten in the house after Sukkot
- Joyous Torah procession in synagogue

CHANUKAH

- Light the menorah, adding one more candle each night until all eight candles are lit
- Give children Chanukah gelt

TU B'SHVAT

- Buy and eat at least one new fruit that hasn't been eaten yet that year and recite the Sheheheyanu
- Eat fruit common in Israel
- Plant seedlings

PURIM

- Fast of Esther day before
- Hear the Megillah at night and during the day
- Send food portion (*shalach manot*) basket to at least one person
- Give charity to at least two people or any organization that gives to the poor
- Have Purim feast in the afternoon

PASSOVER

- Remove any *hametz* from the home, and refrain from eating any for the entire holiday
- Attend a seder the first two nights, and read from the Haggadah
- Eat matzo the first two nights
- Light candles the first, second, seventh, and eighth nights
- Festive meals the last two nights

SHAVUOT

- Light candles both nights
- Kiddush both nights
- Hear the Ten Commandments in synagogue
- Eat festive meal of dairy foods after synagogue

SHABBAT

- Candlelighting before sunset on Friday night
- Festive meals on Friday night, Saturday afternoon, and Saturday night
- Attend synagogue on Saturday morning
- Havdalah ceremony at the end of Shabbat

GLOSSARY OF HEBREW TERMS

Afikomen
A piece of matzo, broken early in a Passover seder and eaten as the final item of the seder meal after dessert.

Ashkenazi
A heritage of tradition associated with Jews of Western and Eastern Europe.

Bereshit
Genesis, the first book of the Bible.

Devarim
The book of Deuteronomy.

Diaspora
The Jewish community geographically outside of Israel.

Gelt (Yiddish)
Money; also the coins given to children at Chanukah.

Hachnasat Orchim
Welcoming guests into one's home.

Haggadah
The Passover service read at the seder table.

Halakah
Jewish law and practice.

Hametz
Leavened grain products like bread, crackers, and cakes that are forbidden to be eaten on Passover.

Havdalah
The ceremony that concludes the Sabbath.

Hiddur Mitzvah
To fulfill the obligation of the Jewish faith (mitzvah) in the most aesthetically attractive manner possible.

Huppah
Traditional wedding ceremony canopy.

Kiddush
A blessing said over wine to sanctify the beginning of Shabbat or a holiday.

Kohanim
Male descendants of the priestly family of ancient Israel; Koheyn is the singular form.

Kohelet
The book of Ecclesiastes, written by King Solomon.

Kol Nidre
The worship service that marks the beginning of Yom Kippur.

Latke (Yiddish)
A potato pancake; a Chanukah delicacy.

L'Shanah Tovah
A Rosh Hashanah greeting meaning "May you be inscribed for a good year."

Maimonides
Jewish scholar, philosopher, and physician who lived in the twelfth century. One of the greatest figures in Jewish history.

Manna
The foodstuff that sustained the Jewish people during their forty years in the desert.

Megillah
Hebrew for "scroll." Generally referring to the biblical scroll of Esther that is chanted on Purim.

Mishnah
The six-book redaction of the core of Jewish oral law, which is the core of the Talmud.

Mitzvah
An obligation of the Jewish faith. Literally means "to bind" to God.

Neilah
The worship service that marks the end of Yom Kippur.

Pareve
Food with ingredients of neither dairy nor animal origin.

Parsha (Sidra)
The weekly Torah portion read in the synagogue every Shabbat morning.

Schach
The branches and greenery that form the roof of the sukkah.

Schnapps (Yiddish)
Whiskey or liqueur.

Sephardic
A heritage of tradition associated with Jews of Spanish origin who come from Africa, the Middle East, southern Europe, and Asia.

Shalach Manot
Baskets of edible gifts, exchanged on Purim day.

Shamash
The candle of a Chanukah menorah used to light the other candles.

Shavuah Tov
"A good week"; the traditional greeting exchanged at the end of the Sabbath.

Shemot
The book of Exodus.

Tashlich
The Rosh Hashanah ceremony of symbolically casting away our sins by throwing bread crumbs into a river or stream.

Tzedakah
Charity. Literally means "justice."

Vayikra
The book of Leviticus.

Yahrzeit candle
A twenty-four-hour memorial candle lit on the anniversary of the death of a loved one.

REFERENCES

Alcalay, Reuven
Words of the Wise
An Anthology of Proverbs
Israel
Massada Ltd., 1980

Donin, Rabbi Hayim Halevy
To Be a Jew
*A Guide to Jewish Observance in
    Contemporary Life*
New York, NY
Basic Books, Inc., 1972

Donin, Rabbi Hayim Halevy
To Pray as a Jew
New York, NY
Basic Books, Inc., 1972

Gervirtz, Rabbi Eliezar
L'Hovin Ul'Hashkil
A Guide of Torah Haskofoh
Jerusalem, Israel
Feldheim Publishers, 1980

Goodman, Philip
The Passover Anthology
Philadephia, PA
The Jewish Publication
Society of America, 1961

Greenberg, Rabbi Irving
The Jewish Way
Living the Holidays
New York, NY
Summit Books, 1988

Katz, Rabbi Mordechai
Menucha V'Simcha
*A Guide to the Basic Laws of
    Shabbat and Yom Tov*
Jerusalem, Israel
Feldheim Publishers, 1982

Kitov, Eliyahu
Book of Our Heritage
Jerusalem, Israel
Feldheim Publishers, 1968

Lubavitch Women
Spice and Spirit
*The Complete Kosher Jewish
    Cookbook*
Brooklyn, NY
Lubavitch Women's
Cookbook Publications, 1990

Miller, Rabbi Avigdor
Kingdom of Cohanim
Comments and Notes on Vayikra
Brooklyn, NY
Self-published, 1994

Miller, Rabbi Avigdor
A Nation Is Born
Comments and Notes on Shmos
Brooklyn, NY
Self-published, 1991

Palatnik, Lori
Friday Night and Beyond
*The Shabbat Experience
    Step by Step*
New York, NY
Jason Aronson, Inc., 1994

Schneerson, Rabbi Menachem
Timeless Patterns in Time
*Chassidic Insights into the
    Cycle of the Jewish Year,
    Volume 1*
Brooklyn, NY
Kehot Publications, 1993

Wineberg, Rabbi Yosef
Lessons in Tanya
*The Tanya of R. Shneur Zalman
    of Liadi*
Brooklyn, NY
Kehot Publication Society, 1993

Wineberg, Rabbi Yosef
Think Jewish
Brooklyn, NY
Kehot Publication Society, 1993

Wouk, Herman
This Is My God
Garden City, NY
Doubleday, 1959

SUPPLIERS

ROSH HASHANAH

Clip Art Books
*Jewish Greeting Cards
for All Occasions*
Ed Sibbett Jr.
Dover Publications, Inc.
31 East 2nd Street
Mineola, NY 11501

SUKKOT

Sukkah Suppliers
The Sukkah Project
4 Pine Tree Lane
Chapel Hill, NC 27514
Phone/Fax: (919) 489-7325
e-mail: stevehen@sukkot.com

Leiter's Sukkahs
1346 39th St.
Brooklyn, NY 11218
Phone: (718) 436-0909

Toll-Free: (800) 422-9199
Fax: (718) 871-7136
e-mail: www.leiterssukkah.com

Feldman and Son
Sukkah Kits
P.O. Box 35001
Los Angeles, CA 90035
Phone: (310) 204-1818

The Esrog Warehouse
78-26 Parsons Blvd.
Flushing, NY 11366
Phone: (888) E-S-R-O-G-I-M
Fax: (718) 380-8463
West Coast: (213) 938-4470

Topiaries (Penthouse Sukkah)
Hinman's Garden Center
175 Albany Turnpike
Canton, CT 06019
Phone: (860) 693-8316

CHANUKAH

Metal Candle Inserts for Menorahs
Kosher Crafts
1270 36th St.
Brooklyn, NY 11218
Phone/Fax: (718) 854-9229
Toll-Free: (800)-9-KRAFTS

Metal Supplies
Allcraft
45 West 46th St. (3rd fl.)
New York, NY 10036
Phone: (212) 840-1860
Toll-Free: (800) 645-7124

PASSOVER

Dinnerware
Stonefish Pottery
30 Arbor St.
Hartford, CT 06106
Phone: (860) 236-9222

Paint for Elijah's Cup
Pébéo of America
Airport Rd.
P. O. Box 717
Swanton, VT 05488
Phone: (819) 829-5012
        (819) 821-4151
e-mail: www.pebeo.com

SHABBAT

Half-pearls for Candlesticks
*(We used two 5-gross bags of
6-mm cultura pearls)*
Elvee/Rosenberg, Inc.
11 West 37th St.
New York, NY 10018
Phone: (212) 575-0767
Fax: (212) 575-0931

ACKNOWLEDGMENTS

It would have been impossible for me to complete a project this complex without the help of many generous and talented people. Thanks to the following:

To my agent, Sarah Jane Freymann, for her enthusiasm and support. She understood immediately what I was trying to accomplish and added some great ideas—and great pages—to this book.

To my first editor at Simon & Schuster, Anne Yarowsky, who worked with me to determine the tone of this work. If not for Anne this would have been a very different book.

To my editor, Constance Herndon, and Assistant Editor Andrea Au at Simon & Schuster, whose discerning eyes left no page of this book untouched.

To Donna Wolf Koplowitz, whose writing was at times moving, at times charming, but always wonderful. She also contributed many creative ideas.

To Dawn Smith, for her extraordinary ability to capture the beauty that even ordinary objects possess. Her beautiful and sensitive photographs never cease to amaze me.

To Stacey Stolman Webb, whose creativity was matched only by her professionalism. For the delicious recipes and wonderful food styling.

To Susan Blubaugh, whose illustrations were able to make complex tasks clear and beautiful at the same time.

To Marilyn Rothstein, who helped me get this idea off the ground.

To Rabbi Shlomo Yaffe, Director, Institute of Jewish Literacy-Chabad House, West Hartford, whose knowledge of Judaism is totally mind-boggling to me. He ensured that the book was in accordance with Jewish law and provided many of the spiritual gems contained in these pages. I was delighted to use some of his creative ideas, too.

To Rabbi Mendel Samuels, who helped with the "Rituals and Prayers" pages.

To Rabbi Yitzchok Adler, for his help with proofreading and the glossary.

To Bill Semrau, without whose help and expertise with the camera-ready production I'd still be working on this book.

To the following people who let me photograph their beautiful homes: Barbara and Stephen Mason, Beth and Don Salzberg, Therese and Tim Adams, and Nina and Brian Lichtenstein.

To Larry Brannon, for schlepping around New York finding props.

To Bruce Komarow, for lending his excellent carpentry skills.

To Mel Tisher, who risked arrest to send me palm tree leaves from Florida.

To the following models: the Goldberg family, Len, Caryl, Evan and Hannah; Lea Brownstein; Jan Anderson and Leah Anderson; Merri Nathan; Ariel Brownstein and Ben Brownstein.

To Hinman's Garden Center in Canton, Connecticut, for the use of their topiaries in the penthouse sukkah.

And last, to my husband, Michael, who drove me and my writer (and good friend), Donna, nuts to make sure that this work would reflect the true greatness of our tradition.

INDEX

You shall love the Lord your God with all your heart, with all your soul, and with all your might. And these words which I command you today shall be upon your heart. You shall teach them thoroughly to your children, and you shall speak of them when you sit in your house and when you walk on the road, when you lie down and when you rise. You shall bind them as a sign upon your hand, and they shall be for a reminder between your eyes. And you shall write them upon the doorposts of your house and upon your gates.

—DEVARIM 6:5–9